Have Your Wedding Cake and Eat It Too!

You Can Be Both Happy and Married

JOEY O'CONNOR

WORD PUBLISHING
NASHVILLE
A Thomas Nelson Company

Published by Word Publishing, a Thomas Nelson, Inc., company, P.O. Box 141000, Nashville, Tennessee 37214, in association with the literary agency of Alive Communications, Inc., 7680 Goddard Street, Suite 200, Colorado Springs, CO 80920.

With special thanks to Robert Llewewllyn Jones for interviewing dozens of guys across the nation and for compiling their insightful, hilarious quotes about marriage in his book, *I Love Her, But . . .* (New York: Workman Publishing, 1996). Many of the chapter-opening paragraphs here are taken from his book.

Library of Congress Cataloging-in-Publication Data

O'Connor, Joey, 1964-
Have your wedding cake and eat it too! : you can be both happy and married / Joey O'Connor
p. cm.
ISBN: 0-8499-3799-X
1. Marriage. 2. Spouses. I. Title.
HQ734 .02899 2000
306.81—dc21 00-036809
CIP

Printed in the United States of America

00 01 02 03 04 05 QWV 9 8 7 6 5 4 3 2 1

To Krista.
You are the light at the end of my carpal tunnel.

Contents

Acknowledgments

Here's a *muy grande* fish taco toast to the great publishing team at Word, Inc. Thank you Lee Gessner, Ami McConnell, Mark Sweeney, Debbie Wickwire, Emily Burton, Tom Williams, Amy Miles, and Mike McDaniel for your enthusiasm, creativity, and fun collaboration on serving a brand new slice of wedding cake advice.

Special thanks to Jennifer Stair for brilliant copyediting work on this book as well as on *I Know You Love Me, But Do You Like Me?* Your insights for detail and structure made both of these books better, faster, stronger than Steve Austin, astronaut, a man barely alive.

May you all enjoy generous helpings of the best wedding cake of all, God's eternal kingdom.

Introduction

Dearly beloved, getting married is not a piece of cake. With hundreds of thousands of engaging wedding choices to make your Big Day one of the best days of your life, your wedding day is more like a NASA space-shuttle liftoff than a simple two-step down the aisle. If you're *a nearlywed* counting down the days to wedding-day liftoff or *a newlywed* who blasted off into the marriage stratosphere a year or two ago, you could say that getting married is truly an experience that is out of this world. Perhaps even an alien experience?

Houston: Marriage Discovery One, this is mission control in Houston. We are T-minus one minute to countdown. Prepare for final liftoff instructions.

Marriage Discovery One: Roger, mission control. The bridal party is buckled in, and all systems are go—*Bam! Bam! Bam!* Houston, you hearing what I'm hearing? Sounds like someone's pounding on the space-shuttle door.

Houston: Roger, Discovery One. We've got a visual . . . looks like someone forgot to let the bride's mother inside. She's standing on the platform, and boy, is she mad! Oops, she just chucked her wedding hat off the platform. We've got a situation developing here.

Discovery One: Houston, the groom admits nothing. Says he's taking the Fifth.

Houston: Roger, Discovery One. We are now T-minus thirty seconds to countdown. Let her in, or she'll be burnt like a side of bacon on takeoff. Suggest you advise the bride.

Discovery One: Houston, we've got a problem. The bride just pinched the groom's oxygen tube, and he's turning blue. She's demanding we open the door for her mother.

Houston: We copy, Discovery One. This is her wedding, you know.

Discovery One: Clarify, Houston: the bride's wedding or the mother's wedding?

Houston: The bride's . . . we think. We are T-minus ten seconds to countdown.

Discovery One: Okay, Darth Mom is buckled in, but she's hotter than my afterburners.

Houston: Roger, Discovery One. Spike her Tang. That'll calm her down. Prepare for countdown. *Ten, nine, eight—*

Discovery One: Oh, geez Louise! Houston, we've got a major system failure here. Our hydraulic warning lights are blinking like a Christmas tree.

Houston: Discovery One, we are holding at T-minus seven seconds to launch. You've got to find the leak, or we're going to scrub this mission.

Discovery One: Got it, Houston. We found the leak in the groom's Depends. The best man is making the change right now. Resume countdown.

Houston: Roger, Discovery One. *Seven, six, five, four—*

Discovery One: Hold it, Houston! I've got the order of service here, and the bride insists on seeing the unity candle before liftoff. Unity candles are against flight rules, aren't they?

Houston: Roger, Discovery One. No open flames on board! It's in the fine print on her contract. Tell the bride she can't have her wedding cake and eat it too. She was lucky to get this launch date. We were booked two years in advance.

Discovery One: Bride says the unity-candle issue is a deal breaker. She wants her deposit back. She and the groom have decided to hit the Velvet Elvis Wedding Chapel in Vegas.

Houston: No can do, Discovery One. She signed the contract. It sticks. Suggest she read *Have Your Wedding Cake and Eat It Too!* for a smoother liftoff into married life. This is one weird wedding party.

Discovery One: We copy, Houston. I've got a funny feeling here. This wedding party reminds me of the *Aliens* trilogy. Where's Sigourney Weaver when we need her?

Houston: Discovery One, we thought this wedding party might be a problem. We saw it coming when they couldn't decide on processional music. Sigourney's here on standby.

Sigourney Weaver: Discovery One, this is Sigourney Weaver. The entire wedding party is not human, repeat, *is not human.* They are aliens wanting to use you as host bodies to multiply their species here on earth. Do not let the aliens go to Vegas. If they get there, we won't be able to tell them apart from the tourists! *Abort mission now!*

Discovery One: Houston! They're coming at us! No! Nooo! NOOOOO!!!

Aliens aside, I know I've got more work cut out for me here than mission control has seen in the past millennium. Whether you're nearlyweds or newlyweds, likely everyone you know is giving you wedding and marriage advice. Everyone and their mother-in-law has a State of "The Union" address for you. They know exactly what you should do.

Enter *moi.* Marriage space explorer extraordinaire.

Maybe you picked up this book because you love wedding cake

and thought this book would give you tips on cake-eating etiquette. But chances are someone gave you this book as a gift for an engagement party, bridal shower, wedding, or anniversary. If you received it at a bachelor party, I'll take that as a compliment.

Before you read on, I already know what you're thinking . . .

Another slice of wedding advice.

Whatever you do, don't bury this book under your *Brides* magazine or fabric swatches.

This book (and your marriage) begs for you to read it.

Have Your Wedding Cake and Eat It Too! is not your typical slice of modern-day wedding advice. You are blasting off on one of the most exciting missions known to mankind. You've heard the advice. You've read the articles. You've attended the premarital counseling, marriage conference, or couples' retreat designed to prepare you for that special wedding kiss and a life of bliss. You want to start the first few years of your marriage on the right track, but I want you to start your marriage off on the *right laugh,* because laughter is the sugar that sweetens married life.

You can have your wedding cake and eat it too if you're willing to learn, grow, stretch, struggle, and make new discoveries as you explore the vast universe of married life. Marriage is a delicious slice of life for every husband and every wife who are ready to have and to hold, from this day forward, for better or worse, for richer or poorer, in sickness and in health, and to love and to cherish every day for the rest of their lives.

Like making a delicious wedding cake, a good marriage takes work, time, and energy. But you can have your wedding cake and eat it too if you're willing to roll up your sleeves and work alongside your spouse to develop the most intimate, loving, and fulfilling human relationship here on earth.

Nearlyweds and newlyweds, I'm excited for you. Guys, I've written this book with you in mind. You'll be glad to know it doesn't come with a ball and chain or a roll of duck tape to rip every single piece of hair off your body. You'll find this book to be very guy-friendly, except the part about Vinnie the garbage man, who makes a killing in the bachelor junk market. Ladies, this book can't help you with floral arrangements, choosing a band, or performing a wedding at sea, but you will find plenty of creative culinary ideas for having your wedding cake and eating it too.

You are beginning one of the most exciting, thrilling, and challenging experiences that this life has to offer. In the following pages, you will learn specific, practical ways for knowing how you can have your wedding cake and eat it too. The first half of this book is devoted to all the craziness nearlyweds go through to get married, and the second half is dedicated to all the wild new discoveries newlyweds experience in the first couple of years of marriage. In each chapter, you'll find a special section called "Together Forever" that will give you the specific principles and practical ideas for developing a together-forever kind of love.

I know you're extremely busy getting ready for your wedding, but you'll finish this book sooner than the time it takes to get your wedding party together for photos. If you're already married, don't let me get in the way of trying to finish your thank-you notes. Take me along on your honeymoon or wedding anniversary. I love a good adventure, and I won't get in the way.

Having your wedding cake and eating it too is an endless universe worth exploring with the one you love.

You two lovebirds sit in back, and I'll steer.

You're in charge of cutting the cake, but make sure my slice is extra thick.

Hurry Up; We're Going to Miss the Wedding!

1

Mawwage . . . mawwage is what bwings us together today.
Mawwage, that bwessed awangement.
That dweam within a dweam.
—*The Princess Bride*

WELCOME TO ARIZONA
THE GRAND CANYON STATE
PHOENIX 151 MILES

Hey, Krista, did that sign say one hundred and fifty miles to Phoenix? What time does Eric's wedding start?"

"Two o'clock, and yes, it's one hundred and fifty miles to Phoenix."

"What time is it now?"

"Twelve-thirty. You want some more beef jerky?"

We had just passed the beautiful resort town of Blythe, California, and crossed over the Colorado River into the Grand Canyon State, where we were headed to a small, Southwest garden wedding in Phoenix, which might as well have been as far away as Philadelphia, Paris, or ancient Phoenicia, which, from what I've heard, was once the bridal-show capital of the ancient world.

"Who moved the state line?" I cried. "We can't be one hundred and fifty miles from Phoenix! That only gives us an hour and a half to get there, let alone try to find where the wedding is! Let me see that map!"

This couldn't be happening. I had in my hands the official Rand McNally Interstate Road Atlas, complete with "easy-to-read, full-color state and city maps" for all fifty states, twelve Canadian provinces, and Mexico—including average sunshine, rainfall, snowfall, temperature, and humidity; a transcontinental mileage chart; state speed laws; visitor's license requirements; and gasoline taxes—and we were still going to be late to Eric's wedding!

"Ugh! We've already been driving for two and a half hours! Krista, this mileage map can't be right. Count up all these numbers between the red dots on Highway 10 starting from here in Quartzsite all the way back to Palm Desert. Maybe there's a misprint."

Like all brave road warriors who have gone before me, I had the trip perfectly planned out. I knew exactly where I was going. I'm not a member of AAA for nothing, you know. Palm Desert to Phoenix was a straight shot, plus or minus an hour or two. There was no way I could miss.

Maybe.

I always throw in a margin of error, especially after the error has been made.

On second thought, I have been known to miss my fair share of flights, freeway exits, buses, trains, escalators, and elevator doors—anything remotely related to public transportation. But this romantic wedding road trip was going to be different. It was just Krista and me, no kids, going to Phoenix for a good friend's wedding. The plan was to leave Friday afternoon, drive a couple of hours to her mom's condo in Palm Desert, go out to dinner, spend fun time alone, go to sleep, wake up, have a leisurely breakfast, hop in the car, get halfway to Phoenix, do a quick mileage check, and suddenly realize *WE'RE GONNA MISS THE WEDDING!*

This punctuality predicament suddenly made me realize how lucky I was to be the proud owner of a four-door Honda Civic. I mean, if I owned one of those *other* foreign cars like a Porsche, Mercedes, BMW, Maserati, Ferrari, or Lamborghini, Krista and I could have waltzed that hundred and fifty miles to the wedding with the top down in the warm May sun, no sweat. But what kind of challenge is that?

I prefer to give my honorable Honda the Japanese stress test by redlining the speedometer so high that the whole car shakes like a big bowl of sashimi sushi in soy sauce. There's nothing more thrilling to me than a reverberating four-door Honda Civic with cloth interior, (I forgot to add) trying to break the land-speed record for cars purchased under ten thousand dollars.

Just think . . . my four-door Honda Civic with cloth interior at 96 mph.

Forget the Phoenix wedding.

We're talking ego trip. Major bragging rights.

"Joey, this mileage map is right," Krista said, bringing me back to road-kill reality. "You'd better step on it, or we're going to miss the wedding."

And so as fast as jumping away from a rattlesnake, I stepped on it. Like the Pony Express of the Old Southwest, I rode my Honda hard. Tall, green saguaro cactuses whizzed by, their prickly needles pointing us in the direction of the dry, rock-scrabbled patch of dirt named Phoenix. From distant peaks, coyotes howled as my gray, four-door Honda Civic with cloth interior ricocheted down Highway 10 like a shining silver bullet blasted out of Wyatt Earp's six-shooter.

Past the Big Horn Mountains. Past Mohawk Pass, Gila Bend, and Casa Grande, which are actually eighty miles to the south on Highway 8, but they're much better sounding Old West names than Wintersburg. I jammed my foot on the Hondarati accelerator as fast as she could go.

"C'mon, Bessie! We can make it," I urged my beast of burden, which was now producing a disturbing throbbing, humming sound similar to what test pilots hear seconds before they eject to safety as their experimental aircraft disintegrates into a million shredded soda cans.

At 1:45, we were still thirty-three miles from Phoenix, and Krista was now changing her clothes in the car. As we blew by eighteen-wheelers driving in the slow lane, Krista almost caused fourteen rigs to jackknife. It was the best road show they'd seen in some time. I don't understand it, but women seem to be double-jointed when it comes to changing clothes in the car. Guys over thirty can barely strap on their seat belts without pulling a rotator cuff and moaning about a bad back. Maybe it's the way women's clothes are designed or the fact that dresses can slip right over their heads, but when I tried to change my pants going 85 mph, the car just wouldn't stay in a straight line. I don't know what the guy's problem was in the lane next to me, but I had my knees on the steering wheel the whole time!

When we finally pulled into Phoenix, we discovered that the state transportation board had set up a conspiracy against us. There were roadblocks and detour signs everywhere! I saw dozens of orange signs that read: "If you're from California, go back home. We don't like your kind!" At this point, my anger level spiked *muy, muy picante* like the little red thermometers on jars of salsa. We did not drive all the way from California to miss a wedding and to nearly kill ourselves in the process.

"Krista, get out the wedding map! Where are we going?"

"It's some sort of public park or library or something."

At this point, since we were in the land of cowboys and Indians, I actually considered pulling over to the side of the road, making a large fire, and sending up smoke signals in the hope that Eric would see our skywriting and send someone to save us from ourselves. I even considered pulling into an Indian gaming casino, but I'd heard that Arizona had banned all indoor smoking, which I figured probably included smoke signals.

We pulled into several gas stations, and I asked for wedding directions in five separate languages: English, Spanish, Hopi, Apache, and Bribery. We were desperate. It was now 2:15, and we were praying that the best man had lost the ring or that a former girlfriend was protesting the wedding.

After zipping, stopping, speeding, and maneuvering like maniacs in the detour-infested streets of Phoenix, Krista and I finally pulled into the library garden parking lot. From inside our air-conditioned, gray, four-door Honda Civic with cloth interior, about one hundred yards away we could see the punctual Phoenix wedding guests sitting in folding chairs and the small wedding party standing at the front of the beautiful desert garden of dirt, cactuses, rocks, cactuses, and dirt.

Yes! We made it! I knew we'd make it!

The wedding guests stood and applauded as Krista and I hopped out of the car and made a mad, frantic dash across the parking lot in the boiling Arizona sun. Much to my wedding-day angst, the applause was not for our arrival, but for another event.

"I'd like to introduce, for the very first time, Mr. and Mrs. Eric Thompson!"

TOGETHER FOREVER

Krista and I missed the wedding, but we didn't miss the wedding cake. By paying careful attention to the map to the wedding reception and by tailgating our friend's car, we made it to the reception on time and without getting lost. The wedding reception was held at a country-western restaurant, where we had a hoot of a good ol' time. Though we missed the wedding kiss, we were able to have our wedding cake and eat it too. As you dig into a delicious slice of having your wedding cake and eating it too, I hope you discover all the joy and happiness available to you in the exciting world of wedded wonder.

Have Your Wedding Cake and Eat It Too! is all about learning how to develop a together-forever kind of love. After all, that's what marriage is all about, isn't it? If you've heard that marriage means you can't have your cake and eat it too, you've heard wrong. Some people may moan about marriage, but you can have your wedding cake and eat it too if you're willing to learn the principles and practical ideas for making your marriage the very best it can be. Marriage is one of life's most fulfilling relationships for men and women who are determined to say "I do" every day for the rest of their lives.

As you're starting this book and starting your new life together as husband and wife, my hope is that you enter your marriage with a powerful sense of hope, enthusiasm, and optimism for spending a wonderful life together. Getting married is a humongous life change, and depending on where you are in your relationship, you could be feeling all sorts of things right now. Whether you're a nearlywed or a newlywed, this book has plenty of wedding cake for everyone. Seconds are included.

- If you're engaged, you could be absolutely zonkers about getting married. You're counting the days and can't wait to be launched into wedded wonder.
- Maybe you're engaged and thrilled to be getting married, but you're also kind of scared and not really sure what married life is all about. You're cautiously enthusiastic.
- Or maybe you're engaged and just scared spitless. It's not that you don't want to be married, but all the planning and preparations and thinking about the future are just a bit overwhelming. You're approaching your wedding day like the long, slow climb up a roller coaster. Click-Click-Click-Click.
- You could be on your honeymoon right now, sitting on a beach in the Bahamas, enjoying one of those exotic blue drinks that costs six bucks because they come with a pink

umbrella sticking out the top. You brought this book along and are curious to see if *laughter* and *marriage* are synonyms or oxymorons.

- Perhaps your first anniversary is just around the corner? You're looking at that freezer-burned carcass of wedding cake and wondering, *What was I doing when I said, "I do?"* You and your spouse want to have your wedding cake and eat it too, but it's been a tough first year, so you're looking for some creative new ways to work out the lumps in the batter.
- Maybe you've been married for a year or two and things are going great, but you want to make sure your marriage keeps growing in the right direction. There's plenty of cake for you too!

Wherever you are in your relationship with the one you love or whatever you're feeling about married life, what you'll discover in this book is that most of your thoughts, feelings, hopes, dreams, frustrations, doubts, and questions about marriage are perfectly normal. Because marriage is such a radical relationship, there are the "high highs" when we feel like we could live on the pure, sweet air of love alone, and there are the "low lows" when we contemplate dressing in black and sitting outside a coffee house in the rain writing depressing existential poetry that no one, not even our dog, would dare to read. Somewhere in the middle of those two extremes is the place where I think most nearlyweds and newlyweds live, and that's where we're headed.

What will make all the difference in your world of wedded wonder is how you develop a together-forever love for your new husband or wife. A together-forever love is being willing to learn more about yourself, your new spouse, marriage, communication, working together, personality differences, emotional and sexual needs, roles and division of labor, conflict resolution, money management, getting along with in-laws, parenting—you name it! Everything that makes up married life needs a together-forever love so you can experience the highest dreams, hopes, and expectations you have for your marriage.

When you're focused on developing a together-forever kind of love, your marriage is the center of life's cinnamon roll. With a together-forever love, you get to toast and to taste the champagne that bubbles up between you. A together-forever love is the juicy, chocolate-dipped strawberry grown in the garden of your friendship. It's the warm his-and-hers bathrobe after a relaxing bath. It's the fresh, hot cup of coffee on a cold morning. It's holding hands as you bask under a burning sun on a deserted beach somewhere in the middle of paradise. It's the warm fire in the hearth as you celebrate your first Christmas together. It's cruising together with the windows down and rocking to music with your feet up on the dashboard. A together-forever love is as certain as the setting sun and as dependable as a large harvest moon. It's the reason you stand at the altar and say, "I do." It's the reason you wake up every morning to a new day of marriage and say, "I will."

Couples who are willing to develop a together-forever kind of love get to have their wedding cake and eat it too because they are willing to say anything, be anything, and do anything to make their marriage the very best it can be. So how can you get started working on a together-forever love in your relationship with your fiancée or your new spouse? I'm glad you asked . . .

If you want a love that's together forever, the first thing you need is a healthy sense of humor. Some people take life and relationships way too seriously. Why have so many couples lost the ability to laugh at themselves and at one another? Laughter is an essential part of staying together forever, because laughter loosens the marriage kinks and knots that everyone gets tangled in. As you read the wild stories in this book, one thing you'll discover is that Krista and I are convinced that laughter makes for a healthy marriage. Every marriage has good times and hard times, but if you're able to laugh about your mistakes, mileage miscalculations, faults, and faux pas, then you'll be well on your way to learning one of the key together-forever principles in this book.

Marriage provides more opportunities for giggles, chuckles, and snickers than anything you'll see on Comedy Central. If you and I can't stand back from our marriages and laugh about our irks and quirks, bumps and thumps, and misfires and backfires, then we'd better check our embalming fluid. A marriage without laughter is destined to flatline on the heart monitor.

As you dig in for a delicious slice of piping hot wedding advice, not only should you be ready to laugh, but you'd better be ready to work. Marriage only rewards those who work at it. To develop a together-forever love, you have to have a strong marriage work ethic. If you want a marriage filled with laughter, joy, celebration, and fun, you have to be convinced that your marriage is worth every ounce of work you put into it.

Every marriage has its problems, conflicts, and frustrations because marriage is made up of two imperfect people trying to make a life together. Throw in finances, personality differences, and individual preferences for whether silverware is placed up or down in the dishwasher basket; then add to the mix 2.5 children, building and balancing a career and home life, sexual and emotional needs, job changes, buying a home, and everything else that falls within the gigantic universe of holy matrimony; and you'll discover that marriage is a whole lot more work than cutting a wedding cake.

That's why the thing you need to understand before you sneak a lick of frosting off the wedding cake is that marriage, above all else, is a learning process. Marriage rewards the couples who work and laugh along the way; but to truly have your wedding cake and eat it too, you have to have a learner's attitude. That means having realistic expectations for yourself as a new husband or wife. It also means having realistic expectations for your new spouse. In your first few years of marriage together, be sure to give one another plenty of growing room. To avoid stunting, every marriage needs plenty of room to grow and thrive.

By giving each other room to grow, you'll be able to step back from your marriage and gain the necessary perspective to measure the areas in which your marriage is strong and the areas in which your marriage needs some work. Living together isn't always easy, which is why it's so critical to understand that marriage is a process. You're going to do a good job as a new husband, and you're going to mess up as a new husband. You're going to do a good job as a new wife, and you're going to mess up as a new wife. And that's okay . . . if you're willing to learn to develop a together-forever kind of love. If you're willing to learn when you make a mistake, you don't have to be too hard on yourself or on your spouse. If your new spouse makes a mistake, you can be generous with forgiveness and both move forward as stronger people with a stronger marriage.

To have your wedding cake and eat it too, all you need is a sense of humor, a willingness to work, and a desire to learn. If you do these things, you'll be well on your way to developing a together-forever kind of love.

A together-forever love is the kind of love that'll take you "till death do us part."

Of course, mileage may vary.

FOR NEARLYWEDS

What types of thoughts and feelings are you having right now about getting married? Which of these things is most important to you: laughter, a willingness to work, or being open to learning in marriage? What are you hoping to get out of this book?

FOR NEWLYWEDS

In your own words, what does a marriage with a together-forever love look like? In which areas is your marriage strong right now? In which areas does it need some attention? Between laughter, a willingness to work, and being open to learning in marriage, which does your marriage need more of right now?

Who Says You Can't Have Your Wedding Cake and Eat It Too?

2

I had been warned by married friends that the cardinal sin, the absolute kiss of death, the one unforgivable offense a man can make in preparing for a wedding is to passively utter, "I don't care," to a question posed by his future wife. Cornflower blue or sea-foam green for the napkins? Of course you care. You care very much.

—Jim Cooper

You fell in love. You got engaged. You set a date. Now you're front-page marriage material. It's one of the most exciting times in your life, but suddenly it seems that everyone you know wants to write the script for your love story. Your well-meaning family and friends, God bless them all, are self-appointed marriage-column editors filling in the blanks of everything you need to know about the rules of engagement, wedding protocol, and marriage myths, maxims, and mottoes to live by. You can't avoid it. Anything you say. Anything you do. Everyone you meet. You get whacked with a wedding whammy wherever you go!

You need more wedding advice like you need five rice cookers or three bread makers or an entire case of KY Jelly to get you through your first year of marriage, right? By now, you've heard and seen it all, haven't you? The "Are-you-sure-this-is-the-one?" interrogations. The "Marriage-is-a-big-commitment" observations. The friendly hugs and shoulder slugs. The future-father-in-law staredown and request for copies of the last three years' tax returns. Your mother's tears and father's fears. The third-cousin-thrice-removed guest list reminders. The blood test. The gift registry hints for making a killing. The bridal shower ideas. Tasteless ball-and-chain jokes. Advice on how to handle wedding coordinators on schnapps. Polite suggestions for wedding-chapel seating assignments that will keep you in the family will. The politically correct rehearsal dinner in-law instructions. The wedding night lovemaking preparations, potions, and positions. The where-to-go-on-your-honeymoon suggestions. The how-to-get-through-the-first-year-of-marriage recommendations. And last, but not least, the dire warnings of cataclysmic doom, should you fail to heed any and everyone's insightful words of wisdom regarding what you must do for your Big Day and every day that follows your Big Day, more commonly known as marriage.

You *must* do this. You *must* do that.

Everybody is *MUSTING* on you!

Be encouraged; you're not alone. The following list, featured on The Ultimate Wedding Web site (www.ultimatewedding.com), represents the top forty frustrations faced by brides and grooms who are sick and tired of having other people shove their wedding cake down their throats:

1. You MUST ___________ (fill in the blank).
2. You cannot use black as a color.
3. Black-and-white weddings look awful in pictures.
4. You must follow tradition.
5. You must make everyone happy.
6. You must wear white.
7. You must wear a veil.
8. You must serve alcohol.
9. You must have dancing.

10. You must have a male relative "give you away."
11. You must have white cake with white frosting.
12. You must have attendants.
13. You must invite everyone your mother-in-law wants!
14. It's not really a wedding if you (or unless you) ________.
15. You must wait until the oldest is married first.
16. You must have a long engagement.
17. You can't be married the same year as another sibling.
18. You must have all the people who ever asked you to be in their wedding in yours—no matter how large it becomes.
19. You must invite ________!
20. You must do what will make your mother happy.
21. You must follow etiquette by the book.
22. You must attend a bridal show.
23. You should not include your fiancé in the wedding plans—this is *your* wedding.
24. You must go to premarital counseling.
25. You should not let the groom go with you for your dress, but you must go with him for his tux.
26. You must do everything just like ________ did.
27. You must have kids in the ceremony.
28. You must address your invitations by hand.
29. You should not have a cash bar.
30. The bride and her family must pay for the entire wedding.

31. You should never start to plan too soon.
32. You must have a wedding coordinator.
33. You must invite everyone you know, including people you haven't seen since they came to your christening.
34. You must have wedding "colors."
35. You must have *all* the siblings and their spouses as attendants.
36. Your female attendants must wear matching dresses.
37. You should not have different shades of white; they will look terrible in the photos.
38. You can't put THAT on your invitations!
39. You must be careful not to read too much etiquette advice—you'll go crazy!
40. You must have the ceremony in a church!

Have you ever stopped to consider that some married people are working on your marriage more than they're working on their own marriages?

Hear me as a different voice. I beg of you.

Brides, you don't have to tell me. I'm painfully aware that I'm fiercely swimming upstream against everything you've already read in bridal magazines. I mean, who could compete with sensational marriage quizzes and intriguing wedding tests like:

- *When He Pops the Question, Does His Snap and Fizzle Make You Sizzle?*
- *How to Show Mr. Right When He's Wrong and Make Him Love You for It!*
- *1003 Ways to Make Him See Stars on Your Honeymoon!*

- *Hassle-Free Ideas for Getting Along with Mothers-in-law and Parole Officers*
- *Razor Stubble and Toilet Seats: Putting a Lid on Your Hubby's Bathroom Behavior*
- *Dynamite Ways to Get Your Guy to Open Up without Using TNT!*

By now you've already flipped through a stack of bridal magazines higher than Niagara Falls, which I guess, as a popular honeymoon spot, is some sort of marriage metaphor for taking the plunge. With the permission of my wife and as part of my extensive research for this book, I do sheepishly admit that I actually bought a few bridal magazines to examine the current trends in wedding fashion, style, and taste. After flipping through a few of these doorstops that were thicker than a Los Angeles phone book, I finally understood the implicit meaning of the environmental slogan "Save a Tree."

So not only have you brides and grooms been blasted with marriage-preparation advice from family, friends, and bridal magazines, you've probably had a few premarital counseling sessions with a so-called marriage expert who has given you all sorts of marriage and personality inventories that ask silly questions to make sure the Groom of Gloom and Doom doesn't marry the Bride of Frankenstein. My bride and I never bothered with those things. Heck, isn't that what our SATs were for? Besides, I'd heard those marriage inventories were filled with very difficult trick questions like:

- *When you were single, what side of your single bed did you sleep on?*
- *When a woman cries, do you know you're wrong or do you instinctively say, "Okay, I'm wrong! I'm wrong!"*
- *How do you know the man you're marrying is not Hannibal Lecter?*

I'm here to tell you what practically everyone else has forgotten to tell you.

Your self-appointed wedding consultants, coordinators, and counselors have been too busy instructing you about the finer points of sturgeon cheese loaves or how to get groomsmen properly groomed or how to prevent a jilted long-lost lover from storming the church, racing down the center aisle with a crazed look, and screaming, "Stop the ceremony! Hear my case as I profess my love and protest this union!"

Those wedding tips are important, but wedding hijackings aside, the first place to properly prepare for a wedding and for married life is to examine the messages you received as a child from your parents. When you were young, your parents told you lots of things. Most of their words helped you become the normal, well-adjusted, functional, and contributing member of society that you are. But some of their messages didn't make sense to you as a kid. The words and phrases your parents used were just plain crazy. For nearlyweds and newlyweds, these same messages can be severely harmful if used during the engagement period and the first few years of marriage. The crazy things your parents said to you are the same crazy things their parents said to them, which will be the same ridiculous things you say to your children unless you do something about it.

As husband and wife, your mission in life is to break this vicious cycle. Wrongly assimilated, the crazy things your parents said to you do not and cannot help prepare you for your Big Day. It doesn't matter whether you are the bride or the groom, these insidious phrases will only get you into big trouble with the person you've promised to hang out with for the rest of your life. You can truly prepare for a lifetime of wedded wonder by growing up and away from saying to your spouse what your parents said to you. Let's take a look under the hood and see what this engine trouble is all about.

Don't Make Me Stop This Car! Once a couple gets engaged, a car is no longer used for making out but reverts to its original purpose—

namely, transportation. Engaged couples have an exhaustive list of meetings and appointments with party planners, churches, wedding reception sites, and all vendors who play a role on their Big Day. It is during these joyous, lighthearted, happy periods of travel to and from wedding-planning meetings that couples typically argue, fight, or (in premarital counseling parlance) "agree to disagree even though I know I'm right."

When an argument escalates and the cruising temperature inside the former make-out mobile reaches the boiling point, if you are the driver, I do not advise saying what your father said when he was ready to blow the roof off the family station wagon. "Don't make me stop this car!" is a driving ultimatum that will slam the brakes on resolving the conflict in a healthy and constructive manner.

What Part of "No" Didn't You Understand? Guys, take it from the legions of married guys who have gone before you: If you want to have a smooth engagement, you say yes when she wants you to say yes, and you say no when she wants you to say no. When she wants you to fall over backward over her choice of china settings, you fall over backward. When she doesn't like the caterer's sampling of shrimp kabobs and bacon-wrapped scallops, you hate those disgusting kabobs with all you have in you. But whatever you do, don't say no and then try to explain yourself.

If You Want to Cry, Go to Your Room and Cry! I seriously doubt the sincerity of any engagement in which a guy fails to make his fiancée cry. When a guy makes his fiancée cry, the worst thing he could possibly do is to send her to her room to cry. But, being a guy, I can understand why a guy would say exactly what his dad said to him. When women cry, guys don't know what to do. We just don't get it. When women cry, we fall apart. We say what we think without thinking about what we're saying. We like to push and prod and prove our point, but we are rendered absolutely defenseless when the love of our life starts to rain buckets from heaven. That's why we only compound the problem when we add, "You can come out of your room when you're ready to stop crying and solve this like a man."

Eat Your Dinner; There Are Starving Kids in the World! The rehearsal dinner is a wonderful time for cheerful toasts and lighthearted roasts, but it's no time to get preachy. In a traditional wedding, the groom's family pays for the rehearsal dinner, but a prospective groom shouldn't worry about losing face if his bride-to-be doesn't clean her plate. The closer a couple gets to their wedding day, the more a woman is concerned about her weight. If she happens to pass out during the ceremony, it's not because she is swooning with love; it's because she's been on a birdseed-and-water diet for the past two months. Using guilt about the plight of millions of starving children to get her to eat her rehearsal dinner will be tough for her to swallow and will leave you both with a bad case of interpersonal indigestion.

You're Grounded for Life! Ladies, if you tell your fiancé he's grounded for life, you can forget about that honeymoon in Tahiti. Wasting expensive airline tickets by putting your groom on restriction just isn't worth it. Though your parents may have used this authoritative power phrase, it's destined to backfire on you—especially if your guy has cable, ESPN, and Internet access in his room. You want him to think, to believe, and to know that all he needs in this life is *you!* If he's grounded for life, you give him the edge on entertaining the terrible idea that coachpotatodom isn't as bad as it's made out to be.

You Can't Have Your Wedding Cake and Eat It Too! The centerpiece of every traditional wedding is the wedding cake. A wedding without a wedding cake is like a wedding without, well, dessert. For all the time, emotion, and energy that goes into planning a wedding, what bride or groom doesn't have the right to dig into their own wedding cake? If you tell your prospective bride or groom that they can't have their wedding cake and eat it too, that is a prenuptial faux pas on par with a groom dropping his bride across the threshold of married life.

That kind of behavior gets you booted out of weddings and sent to the back row of Premarital 101.

TOGETHER FOREVER

When I went to weddings as a kid, I devoured as much free cake as I could shove into my fat little face with two fists. Then, sometime during late adolescence, my parents began to tell me I couldn't have my cake and eat it too. At first, I was quite confused. Suddenly, *The Twilight Zone* theme song echoed throughout the walls of our house. The hairs on the nape of my neck prickled like hundreds of sharp, tiny needles. A cold chill reverberated throughout my body as a leery, eerie thought slithered in my mind: *When was the last time I saw my parents eating cake? They always finish their coffee, but what about their cake? Seven kids. Seven birthdays. But when was the last time I saw them actually eating cake?*

As I grew older, other people I knew began to spout this ridiculous, outlandish phrase. College professors. Bosses. Highway patrol officers. Even my very own friends. They'd all received the same frightening message—*you can't have your cake and eat it too!* Those terrible words hurt us as children. Just think what they do to newlyweds intoxicated with one another, eager for love's first bite? Tell me, how could anybody sit down for a thick, rich, delicious slice of gastro-elation so divine that everything in us pants and screams for a second and third piece, only to be tongue-lashed with such wicked, wounding words? I'm here to announce freedom to cake lovers! You *can* have your wedding cake and eat it too, but before you dig in, it might be helpful to examine what you believe about marriage.

Everybody has certain beliefs about marriage. Some people believe marriage is a wonderful opportunity for a man and woman to develop an intimate, lifelong bond with one another. Other people believe marriage is the Bermuda Triangle of relationships, and only the lucky make it out alive. Some people believe marriage is a sacred trust broken only by death. Others believe marriage is merely a social construction held together by a worthless piece of paper. Some believe marriage is ordained by God. Others believe marriage is simply a place to share designer genes. Some people believe the marriage commitment is what you make it. Others believe the marriage commitment is optional, and if you want, you can break it. Some people believe marriage is the starting point for making a family. Others believe marriage is the place to begin redefining the family. Some believe marriage is a covenant; others believe it's a contract. Some believe marriage is a partnership; others believe it's teamwork. Whatever you believe about marriage, one thing is certain: What you believe about marriage and relationships will have a strong impact on how you live out your marriage commitment to your spouse.

By and large, most of what we believe about marriage is shaped, developed, and influenced by the people who raised us. Just as our parents told us crazy things like a telephone would have to be surgically removed from our ears or how our faces would stay like that if we made that awful expression one more time, our parents left permanent marriage messages on our hearts. Good or bad, right or wrong, together forever or divorced and remarried six times, we all learned about marriage and relationships from our parents. So as we talk about developing a together-forever kind of love, it will be helpful for your marriage if you think about what you learned from your parents' marriage. Like all of us, your parents aren't perfect, but discovering how your parents' relationship impacted your view of marriage will definitely help prepare you for where you're going and who you want to be.

Understanding Your Past. Your parents had a huge influence on the person you are today and, in many ways, will play a big influence in your marriage both now and in the years to come. What was it like growing up in your home? Did you have a happy childhood or an unhappy one? Did you go on family vacations? Did your parents come to your school activities and athletic events? What was the family atmosphere like in your home? Was it warm? Nurturing? Fun? A place of belonging and comfort? Or was it indifferent? A roller coaster of conflict and peace? Was it cold? Unsafe?

If you were to describe your parents' marriage in three words, how would you describe it? How did your parents treat one another? What was their style of communicating? How did your parents handle conflict? What were their attitudes about family, work, church, money, sex, and getting along with others? Were your parents affectionate with each other? Did they treat each other with honor and mutual respect?

All of us have said at one time or another that when we get married and have kids of our own, we're going to be completely different than our parents. In some cases, this is true; in many cases, it's not. In love and marriage, most of us go back to what we know, and the majority of what we know has been modeled by our parents. Understanding your upbringing can have a dramatic influence in how you approach your new role as husband or wife.

Learning in the Present. Taking time to talk about the messages and values you learned from your parents can greatly help you understand the values and positive character qualities you want to bring into your marriage. What did you learn from your parents' marriage that is worth bringing into your marriage? What were your parents' positive character qualities? What would you do differently than your parents? Were there any unresolved conflicts that you would have liked to have been resolved? If your parents were divorced, how did their divorce affect you? How did it influence your attitudes about marriage? What did you learn from their divorce?

Growing Together for Your Future. Communicating with your future husband or wife about your family upbringing is an important way for both of you to understand each other's histories. Every childhood is shaped by high points and low points. Many of the most common marriage struggles (communicating wants and needs, handling conflict, dealing with money problems, etc.) go back to unresolved conflicts of childhood. Talking about how your parents shaped you into the person you are today will give you a better understanding of your personal strengths and weaknesses. By understanding each other's past, you'll be better equipped to handle your marriage in the present.

The good news of this book, whether you had a great childhood or a lousy one, is that you can have your wedding cake and eat it too by learning the practical principles for developing a together-forever kind of love. Your challenge is to grow together with your spouse by creating an intimate, loving marriage through consistently honoring and serving one another as husband and wife. The future is yours. And just in case your parents were wondering . . . This book won't shoot your eye out.

FOR NEARLYWEDS

Take some time to read over the questions in the previous paragraphs. Talk about how your family influenced your attitudes about marriage and relationships.

FOR NEWLYWEDS

Every marriage needs positive role models. Who are the positive marriage role models in your life? What can you do this week to put into practice some of the positive things you learned from your family or a family you love and respect?

Dressed for Marriage Success

3

You should never kiss a girl unless you have enough bucks to buy her a ring and her own VCR, 'cause she'll want to have videos of the wedding.

—ALLAN, AGE 10

I am absolutely shocked at the disparity between the gargantuan size of bridal magazines for women and the twenty-page afterthought of an advertising supplement for guys called *Grooms.* When I went out to buy my first bridal magazine, it was so big I needed a forklift to get it into the trunk of my car. Not only did I nearly throw out my back trying to get it up the stairs and into my office, but I seriously considered adding steel reinforcements to the framing of our house if, by chance, I had the urge to buy ten or more of these magazines, like the average American bride.

All that work of lugging one bridal magazine up to my office was worth it, though. I had a scream of a good time reading the *Grooms* advertising supplement. I'd never seen nor heard of anything like it in my life. As I flipped through the various advertisements, I came across more blatant, outlandish advertising lies than I'd read in a lifetime. I had a hoot reading the exact opposite of what every guy knows to be true about getting married. Get a load of these pitches:

Get together, get comfortable, and register for the gifts you really want. In a guys' magazine? About the only thing guys get to register for is the draft.

The next ad read . . .

The gift registry for guys . . . It's your wedding too! This is a terrible myth that has gotten a lot of engaged guys into really big trouble. Aside from *engagement* being a military term, any guy who tries to assert that "it's his wedding too" by trying to usurp what has already been registered in his fiancée's mind since her childhood dream of planning her wedding is asking for serious double-bubble trouble.

I couldn't believe what the next ad said . . .

Accessories are a guy's best friend. Who writes this stuff? If you're a woman, I would seriously reconsider marrying a guy whose best friend is a pair of cuff links.

The last and most ridiculous ad showed a sexy single woman hugging a white bath towel. The ad read . . .

Next to you, the only thing that will feel softer against his body tonight is our tuxedo. Now I am ready to admit that I am fashionably challenged, but the last thing a guy cares about is how soft his tuxedo is. When a guy goes shopping for a tuxedo, he goes exactly where his fiancée tells him to go and wears exactly what his fiancée tells him to wear. Why is this true? Because the whole wedding theme hinges on how Priority A, the bride's wedding gown, matches with Priority E, the groom's tuxedo. Now you're probably thinking, *Well, why isn't the groom Priority B, as in A and B?* It's because I've thought about this wedding-fashion stuff for a long time, that's why. In strict fashion prioritization, the groom is Priority E because the bridesmaids' dresses are Priority B. Anyone with half a fashion stitch in 'em knows that the bridesmaids' dresses must complement, or should I say, illuminate the bridal gown. Priority C, therefore, falls to the ring bearer's and flower girl's outfits, because everybody loves to watch the adorable little flower girl drop rose petals down the center aisle of the church as the ring bearer stands in the back refusing to walk down the aisle with another girl, picking his nose like all real guys do in times of deep introspection.

Priority D then falls to the minister's suit, which, in most cases, will be a tasteful black or blue that complements the ring bearer's and flower girl's outfits. If the minister happens to wear a multicolored robe, that presents a particular wedding-ceremony conundrum and can easily throw off the whole wedding theme. The minister's suit is Priority D because he faces the audience the whole time. The groom's tuxedo is a lower priority because the back of his tuxedo is nothing thrilling to look at. But the audience can marvel at the intricate design on the back of the bride's wedding gown, Priority A, as well as the sweeping train that cascades down the altar steps. Or if the wedding gown is backless, the audience can look for any unusually large moles on the bride's back that happen to be shaped like the state of Florida.

This finally brings us to Priority E, the groom's tuxedo, which will include the groomsmen's tuxedos as well. It is essential that the tuxedos worn by the groom and groomsmen illuminate the bridesmaids' dresses. For you visual learners, think of this fashion prioritization in terms of a crescendoing effect. Everything builds toward the wedding gown as the key focus of the ceremony.

Priority A: Bride's Wedding Gown

Priority B: Bridesmaids' Dresses

Priority C: Ring Bearer's and Flower Girl's Outfits

Priority D: Minister's Suit

Priority E: Groom's Rented Tuxedo

Once you understand where a groom falls in the wedding-theme fashion prioritization, you can see why his mission impossible is to get in and out of that tuxedo store in less than an hour. The last thing he's thinking about is whether his tuxedo feels anything like a woman's body. A tuxedo is only an expensive piece of clothing that looks good on the outside but on the inside, we know, holds more sweat than the Hoover Dam. Do guys really stand around in tuxedo stores and discuss how tuxedos feel in comparison to a woman's body?

"I can't wear this tux. It feels like I'm hugging my grandma."

"Get this wretched thing off of me. It reminds me of slow-dancing in eighth grade with Lydia Hawksendorf!"

"I refuse to wear any tux that reminds me of my ex-girlfriend who left me for Fabio romance novels."

Guys just don't think like that.

I gotta admit it, guys, I mean *grooms,* we've got it pretty easy. When you get engaged, about the only real wedding responsibilities you have are to get a tux, go to the wedding rehearsal, and show up to the church on time on the right day—dressed, showered, and shaved. It's your final slam dunk of single life.

To make it to the altar in the appropriate attire, all you have to do is go to a tuxedo rental store, pick out the monkey suit currently in style, slap down a hundred bucks, and make sure your groomsmen do the same. If the groomsmen don't do it when you tell 'em to, you can force 'em to wear powder-blue, carnation-scented, seventies-era ruffles. (Better run that one by your fiancée first.)

Now getting a tux can be more difficult than it sounds, especially if you're getting married in your hometown. If you and your fiancée are high-school sweethearts, you'll probably go to the same tux store you went to for your high-school prom. If you're not careful though, the same old, grouchy Hungarian tailor who worked there when you rented a tuxedo for your high-school prom might just rent you the same tuxedo. If you arrive at the church on your wedding day failing to notice that this is the same ugly maroon tuxedo you wore ten years ago, don't be surprised if your bride-to-be experiences violent, hallucinatory flashbacks of the vampish tramp you took to the prom instead of her. Instead of beginning a new life together, you might now be in danger of your life.

Why are you wearing a maroon tuxedo? You know I've always hated maroon! Today is our wedding day, and our wedding color is PEACH MELBA CHIFFON, not maroon! Just can't get Valerie the Vampy Tramp out of your mind, can you? Bet you're still thinking about her matching maroon prom dress, huh? Here, let's tighten your cummerbund a bit . . . around your neck!

Renting a tux does have inherent wedding-day dangers.

Whereas renting a tux for a guy is approximately the same difficulty level as ordering a pizza with half black olives and half Hawaiian pig, many women experience the polar opposite in selecting a wedding gown and the accompanying bridesmaids' dresses. Within a very short period of time, women face two of the most vexing choices of their life (which is more difficult, I'm not sure): choosing a wedding gown and choosing a husband.

The verdict isn't in, but many married women do attest that it's easier to alter a wedding gown than it is to pin a guy down, much less try to alter him in any way. But in defense of married and engaged guys brave enough to read this book, marriage is not fun if you're always walking around on pins and needles. In my extensive nearlywed and newlywed research, I was absolutely amazed at the myriad choices, options, and decisions women have to make in selecting the one wedding gown that will reflect their best side from all sides.

Difficult decisions aside, being bride for a day does have its advantages.

Framed by gorgeous hair, riveting eyes, sparkling jewelry, and an intoxicating, light scent of sweet perfume wafting through the air, a bride in a beautiful wedding gown does crazy things to guys. Guys choke on their chewing gum. They bump into each other with the hot coffee and wedding cake they're carrying to their dates. Jaws crash like bricks to the ground. Neck collars steam with Vesuvian volcanic activity. Gumby eyes give googly stares. Married guys are slapped in the face and told to snap out of it.

Wear a gorgeous gown, and you'll give guys whiplash, snapping their necks in midstep as they pass out on the church floor, their last thought a curse of condemnation for never calling you back after the first date. Abandoned to a bleak eternity of living without you, your bridal gown will burn their eyes with envy at the foolishness of their fickle ways. Searing their minds with the image of you standing at the altar with someone else, your wedding gown will serve its just desserts as you cut the cake with the one man worthy of your love. All other suitors are cut to ribbons.

Grooms in rental monkey suits will never fully appreciate the significance of the wedding gown. When a groom and his herd of gorilla boys stand at the altar, nobody does anything but glance for a second. The groom's momentary appearance is simply that: a momentary appearance. The audience looks at the groom as a passing afterthought and collectively thinks, *Oh, that's nice.* Then, the whole crowd *looks away from the groom,* their eyes staring at the back of the church.

At this point, the groom is just a notch above the wedding-status level of his third-grade candle-bearing cousin, because the groom's appearance is simply the metaphorical torch for the moment everyone has been waiting for: *Le Gran Entrance.*

The grand entrance of the bride in her wedding gown is the centerpiece of the wedding celebration. The bride in her wedding gown is the quintessential focus of wedding-day couture. From contemporary to traditional to romantic to classical to simple yet elegant, a bride's wedding gown wins her the oohs, wows, and aahs of a hushed, expectant crowd awaiting her grand entrance. The generous, graceful smile of a striking bride in her wedding gown is the popping of the champagne cork, announcing to all gathered guests, "Let the wedding games begin!" It is the premiere fashion statement finale for fairy-tale fantasies and Cinderella child's play. The wedding gown sounds the wedding bells, ignites the unity candle, and melts strong fathers into sobbing babies. It is the first fashion beat of Mozart's wedding cantata and the attention-snapping drumroll for the newlyweds' first dance. From veil to tiara to train, a woman's wedding gown is the beautiful bouquet of love's finest scent. After the rice has been thrown, the guests have gone home, and the tin cans have made that klinkety-klink hollow rattling sound behind the honeymoon getaway car, a bride in her wedding gown is forever fascinating.

TOGETHER FOREVER

Every morning of your married life, you and your spouse will wake up and decide what you want to wear. If you're a guy, you will open the small military footlocker under your bed, which you received as a wedding gift. Say hello to your new horizontal closet. If you're lucky, someday you might get an armoire, but to find out what an armoire is, you'll have to look up that word in a French dictionary. (I didn't know what an armoire was until I got married; it wasn't on those marriage-preparation vocabulary tests.)

If you're a woman, you'll be delighted to know that you get the closet, the whole closet, and nothing but the closet, which is every newly married man's Nordstrom nightmare. Any remodeling you do in your master bedroom will be to increase the square footage of your closet. Why just last year, Krista and I built a two-thousand-square-foot addition to our master bedroom—a closet.

If your new husband is nice to you and brings you flowers every week, you may consider subletting a two-foot section of closet space to let him hang his shirts. Unless, of course, you're planning on buying him an armoire for his birthday. Forget those baseball season tickets; what your husband needs is a *manly armoire*. It's a guy thing. Definite *GQ* material.

Whether your clothes are in the closet or under the bed, the most important decision you make every morning is not what you're going to wear on the outside, but what you're going to wear on the inside. *What you're going to wear on your heart.* It's getting your heart fitted for what matters most in marriage. It's dressing for marriage success. Like having the right ingredients for a delicious wedding cake, dressing for marriage success begins with understanding that marriage is, first and foremost, a matter of the heart. A marriage is defined by what's on the inside of a person rather than what's on the outside.

Think about the married couples you know who look sharp, dress sharp, and are sharp. They're dressed every day for success. They have a lifestyle defined by their *successories.* An attractive, large home. The Beamer. The Porsche. The Hummer in the driveway. Expensive jewelry. Exotic vacations. Lots of toys to play with. A thick stock portfolio. A fat checking account. There's nothing wrong with successories, but external, material items can't create a happy marriage. You can't get relationship success by material success, because you can't fill an internal need for love with an external thing like an armoire. If you want to dress for marriage success, you must understand that real, lasting marriage success begins with your heart.

If you're going to have your wedding cake and eat it too, you've got to be wearing the right wedding attire. Once the bridal gown has come off and the tuxedo has been returned to the shop, you've got to wear what's right for your heart and what works for making marriage last in a wonderful and meaningful way. You can have your wedding cake and eat it too by choosing to clothe your heart with the character qualities that will help you develop a together-forever kind of love in your marriage.

How do you live out your marriage vows in a way that deepens your relationship and plants your marriage on the bedrock of solid commitment? If you're going to enter the world of wedded wonder, you dress your heart each day with character qualities that will draw your spouse to you. You go for relationship success first before any other type of success. Just the other day, I was flipping through one of my favorite books and found this string of pearls that looks beautiful on any heart. If you want to dress for marriage success, try these words of wisdom on for size. They are just what every marriage needs:

> Therefore, as God's chosen people, holy and dearly loved, clothe yourselves with compassion, kindness, humility, gentleness and patience. Bear with each other and forgive whatever grievances you may have against one another. Forgive as the Lord forgave you. And over all these virtues put on love, which binds them all together in perfect unity. (Col. 3:12–14)

Marriage is a matter of the heart. Getting to the heart of marriage can only happen when you intentionally focus on developing the character qualities that can keep your relationship together forever. Before any other type of success, you must make it your highest priority to focus on dressing your marriage for success. A marriage dressed for success is a marriage of quality, intimacy, meaning, and richness characterized by . . .

Being chosen: Recognizing your deep need and desire to choose and to be chosen.

Holiness: Understanding true "wholeness" comes from being in right relationship with God.

Compassion: Sharing each other's struggles and hardships with all comfort.

Kindness: Showing concern for the things that are important to your spouse.

Humility: Being able to admit your mistakes and receive constructive criticism.

Gentleness: Being considerate and thoughtful, not harsh, in words and in actions.

Patience: Keeping a calm spirit when it would be easier to fly off the handle.

Support: Doing whatever you can to build up and encourage your spouse.

Forgiveness: Being generous with pardon even when you don't feel like it.

Love: Freely receiving what comes from God and then selflessly giving it away.

Unity: Being one in spirit and purpose; allowing nothing to divide your marriage.

These are the character qualities that make or break the wedding cake. These are both the rich chocolate core and the frosting on the cake. This is the real stuff that makes a marriage last, the stuff that creates a together-forever kind of love that enables you to make it through wherever your marriage takes you.

If you're going to dig deep in your marriage, these are the qualities to chew on. Make the daily decision to dress for marriage success by putting these qualities into practice. Whether you're a nearlywed or a newlywed, these are the qualities that brought you together in the first place, and they will make a powerful difference in how you deepen your love for one another as you take off for your honeymoon and into the wild world of wedded wonder. The best thing about these qualities is that they're yours forever.

They're a perfect fit for whoever wants to wear them.

Better yet, you won't have to return them the day after your wedding.

FOR NEARLYWEDS

Out of the character qualities listed above, which ones drew you most to your fiancée? Which qualities do you think your fiancée admires most in you? Which qualities do you think will make the most difference during this busy season of planning your wedding? Why? (Be specific.)

FOR NEWLYWEDS

Which of the character qualities listed above do you demonstrate the most so far in your marriage? Which ones do you need to work on? What can you do this week to put one of these character qualities into practice? (Be specific.)

Get Extremely Married

4

Marriage is when you get to keep your girl and don't have to give her back to her parents.

—Eric, age 6

Hang around the wedding circuit long enough, and you'll discover that offbeat, alternative weddings are pretty hip these days. Traditional is out; edgy is in. Some couples just can't stomach the idea of a staid, traditional wedding with all its pomp and circumstance, frilly dresses, and goose-stepping wedding coordinators who'll beat them within one inch of their life if they don't stand exactly where they're told to stand.

The couples who want offbeat, nontraditional weddings are usually, but not always, the same couples who meet while marveling at the beauty and simplicity of the food-chain cycle in great white shark cages off the Great Barrier Reef in Australia. While a hungry, twenty-foot female great white repeatedly rams the cage like a first-time mom with a stroller at a Gymboree sale, the couple jots down flirtatious notes on their grease boards. Nonplussed by the great white's ferocity, the savageness with which it attacks the cage, and the fact that the shark has just swallowed three eight-foot stainless steel bars from the cage, the couple makes plans right then and there to go on a belly-crawling, spelunking exploration in search of massive guano mounds deposited by the docile, yet regular Australian fruit bat.

Extreme enthusiasts—men and women who meet while jumping out of planes, climbing the Tierra del Fuego tip of South America, windsurfing across the English Channel, bungee jumping off playground equipment at local parks, snowboarding down avalanche chutes, surfing on forty-foot waves on the North Shore of Oahu, motorcycling across the Mexican desert, or trying to find help at Home Depot on a Saturday—are the same adventurers who recognize that marriage is the most extreme of all relationships. These nonconformists will do just about anything to stay off the ho-hum, predictable path of the oft-trodden, carpeted church aisle. If it's not wet, freezing, vertical, overhanging, dangerous, underground, underwater, sweltering, or gravity defying, these extremists don't want to have anything to do with it. These adrenaline junkies want to get married, *extremely married.* They want to skyrocket out of singlehood with a blast. A horizontal, straight church aisle at tepid room temperature filled with people who aren't in scuba gear just doesn't cut it. Why walk down an aisle when you can jump out of a plane? If they are committing themselves to one person for the rest of their lives with the vow "till death do us part," then by gosh, they're going to make getting married a death-defying experience.

If you're planning on getting extremely married with an edgy, nontraditional wedding, be prepared for a logistical nightmare. Before you start pushing the wedding invitation envelope by planning a spectacular event, you might want to consider the inherent dangers involved in getting extremely married.

Skydiving Weddings Are Very Expensive. The couple ready to leap into married life needs to know that most skydiving companies won't tell you how much it costs to rent a 747, which is what you're going to need if you're going to book a large wedding with a reputable skydiving company. (They do have minimums, you know.) Skydiving weddings average between two and three hundred guests, so you can just toss out the idea of packing all your family and friends into a single-engine Cessna for your big jump. That means you're going to need jumpsuits, helmets, goggles, and parachutes for every guest, which are expenses not included in the 747 rental. Throw in a day of jump-school training, which also means you'll have to pick up the tab for lunch, and before you know it, your wedding bills are going to spike straight into the stratosphere.

Once the plane door is open and everyone is ready to jump, you'll have to figure out who jumps first. If I were you, I'd have all the wedding guests jump before I stepped an inch outside of that plane. That way you and your fiancée can make sure everyone's chute opens with a *POOF! POOF! POOF!* and you'll know the skydiving company is really as reliable as it says it is.

For the uninitiated, the skydiving wedding looks like a lot of fun, but it's a nightmare on the wedding guests with a fear of flying. If anyone on the plane is afraid to jump, I'd rig a chicken exit by ripping off the bathroom door and replacing it with the back door of the plane.

"You're so scared to jump, you're ready to pee in your pants? See that door in the rear of the plane. That's the bathroom."

If I'm shelling out a few hundred bucks for guests to jump, they're going to jump.

Rock-Climbing Weddings Are Logistically Impossible. For the vertically inclined, a rock-climbing wedding is a great metaphor for climbing on top of each other for the rest of your lives. But what most rock climbers underestimate is just how many people have a terrible fear of heights. Male and female rock climbers think nothing of hanging off a thousand-foot cliff tied together by a thin cord and connected to a few scraps of expensive metal gadgets that are fun to play with in sporting-goods stores. Imagine what your wedding might look like when you lower your ninety-four-year-old Grandma Lowenstein, dressed in a pink Lycra climbing leotard, to your vertical altar one hundred and fifty feet below the edge of the cliff. Like parachutes for a skydiving wedding, you're going to need a climbing rope and harness for every guest, which means you're also going to need someone to belay each and every guest. That automatically doubles your guest list!

Say you have fifty guests hanging off the edge of the cliff while you and your beloved climbing partner tie the proverbial knot. Half of those guests, I guarantee you, will throw up. When your guests start turning green, you don't want to be below these people. Even if it's a windy day, there's bound to be an updraft, so wear a rain slicker and count on getting some on you. You can also plan on a few hysterical guests who can't believe they actually let you talk them into being hung over a cliff like a wet hunk of mackerel on a marlin trawl line. Right in the middle of your wedding vows, the most sacred part of this alpine ceremony, you'll hear bloodcurdling screams of desperation: "Please, please, please, oh please, SOMEBODY PLEASE GET ME OFF THIS MOUNTAIN!" These screams will incite a panic among the rest of the sick and infirm wedding wimps as dozens of your yellow-bellied guests join in, "YEAH, SOMEBODY GET US OFF THIS CLIFF!" "IS ANYBODY OUT THERE!" "LIFE ALERT! HELP, I'VE FALLEN AND I CAN'T GET UP!" Paralyzed by fear, your wedding guests will limply hang on the cliff like twisting sides of beef blowing in the wind. Your belayers will be unable to haul them up, which will create an emergency crisis with the National Park Service, which will be summoned to help save your wedding and your hapless guests. The Park Service rangers will not be happy campers. You need permits for these kinds of outings. Your wedding license will not count.

Snowboarding Weddings Are Downright Dangerous. Unless everyone coming to your wedding is twenty-five and under, you can give up the hope of having a snowboarding wedding on a steep, powdery slope. Most people barely know how to ski, let alone stand on a slick board with one edge and surf down a mountainside following a bride and groom who are catching major air and exchanging rings at the same time. Forget that snowboarding is difficult for your three-hundred-pound Aunt Lorraine or that it's expensive like skydiving and rock climbing: Snowboarding is a lousy way to die.

Skydiving, *splat* . . . you die.

Rock climbing, *splat* . . . you die.

Snowboarding, you die . . . *slowly.*

Say you're a snowboarding wedding guest. You're standing at the top of the mountain, and the wedding party has just taken off down the hill. You ease yourself off a slight incline, get your balance, and off you go. You pick up a little speed—*Look at me . . . this ain't too bad.* You're doing pretty well for the first time, getting down the hill without endangering the lives of others because experienced skiers and snowboarders have enough common sense to stay away from objective hazards like you. You're feeling pretty confident, maybe a little overconfident, then *whoa!* you catch an edge, veer off course, and plow straight into a ten-foot wall of fresh powder underneath the deck of the midmountain ski lodge.

No one comes to your aid because no one saw you enter the wall of snow, which already contains three frozen corpses. Because you can't move forward, backward, sideways, or touch your toes, your snowboard boots are the mountaineering equivalent of Mafia cement swim fins. So, you slowly suffocate as people on the deck directly above you drink expensive cappuccinos and get raccoon-eye tan lines from basking in the sun.

Losing one guest to snowboarding suffocation is not a huge legal liability, but what if, say, one hundred and fifty of your guests are swept up in an avalanche? Now you're talking a class-action lawsuit. Before the snow melts to find all your frozen guests, you'll have more lawyers crashing your reception than vultures hovering over the avalanche site waiting for the spring thaw.

Predicting and preventing an avalanche on your wedding day is next to impossible. If you and your bride want the best powder, you need to be the first on the mountain. If the mountain's going to shrug its shoulders and dump a gazillion tons of snow, rock, and ice on your guests' heads, there's not much you can do to stop it. However, when Aunt Lorraine unleashes an avalanche by displacing a single snowflake on her snowboard, there are a number of safety measures you can take to reach the avalanche victims as soon as possible.

First, instead of providing guests with battery-operated avalanche radio transponders, which emit a beeping signal for locating them, give them kitchen timers. Kitchen timers are much more reliable than batteries, and their distinctive ring will be readily heard by the pack of St. Bernards you rent for retrieving your snow-buried guests. You'll need one St. Bernard per five buried guests. If seventy-five guests get swallowed by the mountain, that means you need fifteen St. Bernards. The tricky thing about working with St. Bernards is that they're the best dogs in avalanche-rescue efforts, and they know it. St. Bernards have a long and proud history of rescuing people in the Swiss Alps. Here in America, these dogs are union. If your avalanche happens during one of their fifteen-minute breaks, your guests can kiss their little air pocket of oxygen good-bye. If those kitchen timers go off when that lead dog blows the whistle, it doesn't matter if you're paying five hundred bucks an hour for those droopy-eyed drool monsters, they're going to crack open those little wooden casks around their necks and pour that martini they've been dying for. If any of your guests manage to dig themselves out, there'll be a green martini olive waiting for them.

TOGETHER FOREVER

If you want to get extremely married, the one thing you need to have in common with extreme sports is an extreme commitment to the one you love. Marriage is one of the most thrilling, exciting adventures you could ever embark on, and that's why I make a big whoop-de-do out of marriage. The wedding celebration will be one of the greatest events of your life together, but that's only the start. What's important to keep in mind as you consider the commitment you're making to your spouse is that as fun and wonderful as the wedding celebration is, a perfect wedding and a beautiful reception with lots of bubbly doesn't and can't create a great marriage. Regardless of the price tag, weddings and receptions are a level playing field for all couples tying the knot. Your wedding and reception can't guarantee a successful marriage.

It doesn't matter if you spend five hundred dollars or five hundred thousand dollars on your wedding, because wedding excesses (or lack thereof) can't make a marriage stronger than a locomotive, faster than a speeding bullet, or able to jump tall buildings (or sofas during halftime) in a single bound. Life and relationships just don't work like that.

A great marriage is the sum total of what a husband and wife make it.

A great marriage doesn't happen by luck, destiny, or finding the perfect person.

A great marriage happens by a husband and wife being extremely committed to one another and to their marriage. Just like it takes a lot of work to make a beautiful wedding cake, it takes a lot of work to make a beautiful marriage. If you want to have your wedding cake and eat it too, both of you must be extremely committed to making your marriage work.

One of my hopes as you read this book is that you hear, again and again, that a great marriage is one of life's greatest gifts. When you get married (or if you already are), every day is a gift you get to share with one another. *You are a gift to one another.* Marriage places you in the position to share your very best hopes, dreams, goals, values, and desires with someone who will share their very best hopes, dreams, goals, values, and desires with you. Marriage gives you the safety and security to open your heart and share your struggles, fears, weaknesses, and limitations. You'll see all of your spouse's strengths, and you'll also see their scars. When you're married, you get to be physically intimate *(yahoo!)*, emotionally intimate *(yeah!)*, intellectually intimate *(whoa!)*, and spiritually intimate *(wow!)*. Marriage is a mirror image of life, but instead of going it alone, you have a spouse who walks alongside you through all of life's ups and downs, triumphs and struggles, victories and defeats. When marriage is really great, life doesn't get any better. That's what you want to shoot for as you start your new life together as husband and wife.

There are so many areas that make marriage the cool, lifelong commitment that it is. Throughout this book, you'll hear me champion what's so great about married life and share a lot of practical ways for starting your first couple of years off right. God has blessed me with a wonderful wife, a truly beautiful person I'm thrilled to spend the rest of my life with. Here's a snapshot of one of the simple joys I find in being married to Krista.

On the mornings I sleep in, I love waking up to the smell of Krista brewing a fresh pot of Starbucks coffee. If we had put as much money into buying Starbucks stock as we have buying their coffee, we'd be millionaires by now. Since Krista and I are major caffeine achievers, many of our dates and times together are centered on going out for a cup of java. We love to sit and talk, read the paper together, or say nothing at all as we bury ourselves in the latest novels we're reading.

Now if I were still single, the only thing I'd get in the morning is a cup of coffee, and I'd have to make it myself. But somehow, a strong cup of coffee doesn't taste as good unless you have someone you love to share it with. When I hear the muffled *wwhhhhrrrr* of the coffee grinder in the morning, I peel my eyes open and think, *Oh, that's a delicious sound.* Making that intoxicating, crunchy roar is my café-mocha wife.

Or when I'm writing in my office upstairs, there's nothing better than Krista coming in with a smile, fresh-baked muffins, and a cup of my favorite French roast. Granted, this happens about twice a year, but hey, I'll take what I can get. Krista has a smile that ignites any of my nearby manuscripts into flames, and the sound of her voice is a welcome interruption in my solitary writer's world.

Coffee aside, one of the qualities I love best about Krista is that I know she is extremely committed to me and to our marriage. We've been married for more than ten years now, and she consistently lives out our marriage vows as if we got married yesterday. If the character qualities I mentioned in the last chapter (being chosen, holiness, compassion, kindness, humility, gentleness, patience, support, forgiveness, love, and unity) were easy qualities to live out in your marriage, then you wouldn't need a very strong commitment to make your marriage work. It's because these character qualities are so challenging to live out that you and I need to be extremely committed to our marriages. These are the indispensable character qualities that enable us to have our wedding cake and eat it too. These are the tools of character that make a good marriage great.

Though we don't rock climb anymore like we used to, Krista has been thoroughly committed to climb with me through all the peaks and valleys our marriage has been through, which has taught me so far that a great marriage isn't a perfect marriage. For as many wonderful qualities that she has, Krista isn't perfect, and she never will be. I'm not the perfect husband, and I never will be either. If we had a perfect marriage, I'd be the first one to mess it up. So I'll settle for a great marriage, but that doesn't mean it's going to come easy. You can't have marital bliss without picking up a few marital blisters along the way. A great marriage is characterized by an extreme commitment to being the best husband or wife you can be.

That makes getting extremely married worth the leap.

FOR NEARLYWEDS

Describe what *commitment* means to you personally. How have you and your fiancée demonstrated a mutual commitment to one another in your relationship so far? What would severely test this commitment in marriage?

FOR NEWLYWEDS

Who has been a healthy model of marriage commitment in your life? What do you admire about this couple's personal character and their marriage? Why are these character qualities so necessary for strengthening your commitment to one another?

Three Weddings and a Funeral

5

It has been said that a bride's attitude toward her betrothed can be summed up in three words: Aisle. Altar. Hymn.

—Frank Muir

If you're in the process of planning your wedding and need to speak to a wedding authority, talk to my dad. He's a wedding coordinator of sorts. My dad can't help you much with wedding music selection; for all I know, he might recommend walking down the aisle to the Archies' *Sugar, Sugar,* Sonny and Cher's *I Got You Babe,* or the soundtrack from *Jaws.* He doesn't throw professional bachelor parties with kegs of beer, balls and chains, shave-the-groom kits, or mud-wrestling matches with surgically enhanced females with names like Mauler, Blade, Destroyer, or Nitro. To my knowledge, Dad's never hemmed a bridal gown nor does he know a lick about wedding dresses. Just the other day, I was flipping through my monthly subscription to *Modern Bride* and quizzed him about the characteristics of popular wedding-dress styles. These are his responses to my haute couture questions:

Antebellum Waist: No wedding bells at the waist. Major wedding faux pas.

Bertha Collar: This collar is big, really big, as in "Big Bertha" big.

Leg-of-Mutton Sleeve: Antivegetarian. A favorite of wolves and coyotes.

Peek-a-Boo Sleeve: Economic sleeve that reveals armpits. Shave, please.

Brush Train: Locomotive that carries paint brushes for new husband to use.

Queen Anne Neckline: A beheading is no way to start your wedding day.

Despite not knowing much about the intricacies of bridal-gown design or cake-cutting etiquette, my dad is well-acquainted with the wallet-piercing phrase "Will that be cash, check, or charge?" In the period of twelve months, my dad accomplished the amazing task of marrying off three of my sisters and one of his sons—me.

Four weddings in one year.

I'd say that makes him a wedding authority.

Of course, he's still working at Taco Bell on the weekends to pay 'em all off.

Anyone remotely related to the wedding industry in my hometown loves my dad.

When he walks through town, my dad's a local celebrity. Complete strangers point, stare, and whisper to one another, "There's the man who paid for three weddings and a rehearsal dinner in one year. He's amazing." Women applaud him, and husbands with two or more unmarried daughters avoid him like they're gonna catch whatever he's got. *Stay away from me and my family, Joe O'Connor. You just keep your distance!*

The mayor awarded my dad the Medal of Honor for his bravery and courage in the face of financial fire. He was also awarded the Purple Heart for the wedding wounds inflicted on his wallet. My dad's the most popular guy on the garage-sale circuit because there's been a garage sale at my folks' home every Saturday for the past ten years. You know how many *National Geographic* magazines you have to sell to pay off three weddings and a rehearsal dinner?

Wearing the Purple Heart does have its downside, though. His neighbors are sick and tired of him knocking on their doors with the two-dollar candy bars he's trying to sell, which has infuriated the kids on local baseball teams because he's cutting into their fund-raising business. Worried about kids with baseball bats, I've suggested to my dad that he should give panhandling a try. I'm convinced my dad would get a lot of sympathy and financial support if he stood at a traffic light with a sign that read:

I PAID FOR THREE WEDDINGS AND
A REHEARSAL DINNER IN ONE YEAR.
PLEASE HELP.

If he'd put on a sad face and wear a battered old tuxedo, my dad would be rolling in so much dough, he wouldn't know what to do with it. Though I can't imagine what kind of financial trepidation my dad faced with each of my sister's wedding days, I do have a little secret to let you in on: My dad didn't get buried with bills like you think he did.

You see, my dad is a funeral director, and he knows how to work the wedding-circuit system. My dad's family has been in the funeral business in Southern California for more than one hundred years. My mom is from Northern California, and her family is also in the funeral business. My mom's parents and dad's parents were friends, and my dad met my mom at a funeral-directors' convention in Fresno. She was modeling burial gowns—Victoria's Secret burial gowns, say no more, *va-va-va-voom!*

Seven children later, instead of getting buried by wedding bills, my dad saved thousands of dollars on my sisters' weddings by a number of insider connections and savvy saving plans that have been passed, or should I say lowered, down through the generations.

First, the year my sisters got married was the year you didn't want to buy a casket from my dad. Prices went up, way up, that year. When customers received their funeral bills, my dad got more than a few phone calls about the 10-percent "wedding tax" that appeared on the invoice. Second, getting the churches for each of my sister's weddings was a snap. Most funerals have a church service, so my dad was able to work his contacts with the funeral coordinators, many of whom also double as wedding coordinators. Thus, the phrase "marry and bury."

Next, my dad was able to lower his expenses by using leftover funeral flowers to decorate the churches and wedding receptions. It was kind of awkward, but each of my sisters carried a large carnation cross for a wedding bouquet. Though my future brothers-in-law protested wearing Bird of Paradise boutonnieres that were still in the pot, that wasn't half as bad compared to all the bridesmaids who had to wear lavender burial gowns. In all three of my sisters' bridal-party photos, you see the same lavender burial gowns. Lavender burial gowns again and again and again. At least they could have dyed them a different color for each wedding.

Getting my sisters to the church on time was no problem. The family firm provided free limousine service. Foreshadowing notwithstanding, the groomsmen loved cruising to the reception in the hearse. I've been sworn to secrecy about what kinds of meals were served at the wedding reception, because this is where my dad saved the most amount of money. Over the years, we've developed a few family recipes and secret sauces, but if I told you the family secrets, I'd have to kill you. Like the Mafia *omertà* oath of silence, our family has a similar Irish oath of silence. Break the oath and you get slowly simmered in a huge vat of mashed potatoes.

While my dad was working on lowering as many wedding expenses as possible, I had my own problems to worry about. Krista and I had a short, I mean really short, three-month engagement. We had a lot to do in a short amount of time, and our "I Do List" rivaled a NASA space-shuttle launch. Though our wedding preparations went relatively smoothly, as the Big Day got closer and closer, a gnawing fear loomed larger and larger inside of me. It was a deep-seated, latent fear that I didn't know existed until I got engaged. And it all had to do with growing up as a son of a mortician.

When I was little, I'd always heard that fun, boppy funeral song "Well, we're going to the chapel and we're gonna get . . ."

I have to stop the song right there because when I was little, going to the chapel meant one of two things. The first was going to church on Sunday. As long as I can remember, my family went to church every Sunday—holidays and holy days included. We were a churchgoing family and, on Sunday, going to the chapel meant going to church. Going to chapel was a part of life. No problem.

But, in my family, going to the chapel was also just a part of doing business. Going to the chapel also meant going to a funeral. So, as you can imagine, whenever I heard that popular funeral song, it scared the living daylights out of me and kept me from ever wanting to get married. You know how that song goes . . .

"Well, we're . . . going to the chapel and we're . . . gonna get bu-er-er-ried. Gee, I really love you and we're . . . gonna get bu-er-er-ried. Going . . . to the chapel . . . of love."

If my wedding day was my burial day, I didn't want no love or no chapel.

I could just see all my groomsmen standing up there in the front of the church, each holding a shovel and devising a scheme for pillaging the spoils of my bachelor junk.

TOGETHER FOREVER

Can you imagine, then, the overwhelming relief I experienced on my wedding day when I discovered that I wasn't going to be buried? *I was going to be married!* Why couldn't I get the words to that song right when I was a kid? I was so glad to lay to rest my fear of *burial by marriage* that I willfully and joyfully stood at the altar. Now I could look forward to getting married because what I thought was *the end* was actually *the beginning*. I wasn't going to be boxed in; I was going to be free to spend the rest of my life with someone whom I had chosen and who had chosen me.

Being chosen.

Isn't that what marriage is all about?

Being chosen by another is the heartbeat of your wedding day. Choosing another person to have and to hold lies at the deepest part of our desire to be had and to be held. Getting married is the choice to choose, again and again, the same person to love every day for the rest of your life. That's what makes marriage an awesome gift and a wonderful privilege: the chance to choose and to be chosen every day of your life. Marriage is a lifelong commitment to make the daily choice to place your life into the hands and heart of your spouse. Being chosen and choosing another is one of the best desserts this life ever offers.

But the way some people talk about marriage today, you'd think they're talking about going to a funeral. It's not uncommon to feel scared, insecure, or unsure about getting married, but don't listen to those who rag on marriage and say it's a death sentence or a life sentence without any possibility of parole. The marriage naysayers talk about your wedding day as if you've got an appointment with the Grim Reaper. Your wedding date is set in stone—a tombstone. "Say good-bye to your former life. Say good-bye to freedom," they cry, as if you were a sheep going to the slaughter. The antimarriage nincompoops spew all sorts of marriage myths and mistakes of others, as if you're going to step on an antipersonnel land mine that will maim you for the rest of your life. They make marriage sound like the afterlife and a lifelong commitment to one person sound like relational slavery.

But I'm here to say that these people, whoever they are, are wrong.

Dead wrong.

Sure, the divorce statistics speak for themselves, and some people have been hurt by a bad marriage or by someone to whom they entrusted their life, but that doesn't mean their story will be your story. The wedding altar is a level playing field. Men and women choose to love, choose to marry, choose to develop a great marriage, choose to make it mediocre, or choose to end the marriage. Husbands make great choices, and husbands make horrible choices. Wives make wonderful choices, and wives make terrible choices. Wealth or poverty, a successful career or unemployment, a good family or a bad family, a college education or no college education, intelligence or lack thereof, beauty or utter ugliness, none of these determine whether a marriage will be successful. What matters are choices. Everybody is given an unlimited number of choices that, ultimately, will determine the strength, intimacy, and longevity of their marriage.

As we dig in for a delicious helping of having your wedding cake and eating it too, you'll see that I won't sugarcoat marriage by saying it's all pie in the sky. An honest, healthy marriage relationship between a husband and wife means that you'll both make a lot of tough choices, many of which we'll explore in this book. Our planet isn't aligned to guarantee that marriage will be a series of easy choices. But, on the other hand, marriage is not a death march for fools in love.

Ever since you were a kid, you had an insatiable need to be chosen and an insatiable need to be loved. Your need to be chosen and loved is the same insatiable need we all have to be chosen and loved because we all want to belong. We want others to know us, to love us, and to accept us for who we are. And, at one time or another, in all of our lives, we've experienced what it's like not to be known, loved, or accepted. Ever get picked last on the playground? Ever get overlooked during Heads Up, 7 Up on rainy days in the classroom? Ever get dumped or jilted quicker than a waste-management truck running late on trash day?

Falling in love, being engaged, and getting married is the wonderful celebration of being chosen. When you know you're chosen, you can relax. You can feel safe and secure. When you know you're loved, you know you belong. That makes you free to grow and to learn and to love as you've been loved. When you and your spouse choose each other daily, you can experience a tremendous amount of security, intimacy, and belonging like never before. Who doesn't love to be at the center of someone else's heart desire?

Many weddings are officiated by a preacher who gives the dazzling-looking bride and groom a sort of spiritual Super Bowl game-day message that tells them to go kick butt and win the game of married life. Somewhere in the pre-vow pep talk, which generally lasts three to forty-five minutes, the preacher inevitably talks about God's love and the importance of keeping love alive in marriage. This is when some guests' minds turn to lukewarm oatmeal, their eyes begin to glaze over, and their stomachs start to wonder if chicken cordon bleu or imitation salmon steaks will be served at the reception. This is unfortunate because what the preacher is talking about is the best meal served of the day. Understanding the importance of God's love and being chosen by God will nourish a marriage like no meal can do. Choosing God's love for your life and your marriage is the Dom Perignon of wedding-day choices. It is a decision you will never regret.

On your wedding day, a lot of people will talk about love and have a lot of opinions about love. Ten to one, I bet you'll get at least one of those Precious Moments knickknacks with the onion-head kids and the inscription that reads, "Love is . . ." But what is true love if it's not first being chosen? "This is love: not that we loved God, but that he loved us and sent his Son as an atoning sacrifice for our sins. Dear friends, since God so loved us, we also ought to love one another" (1 John 4:10–11).

Before you were ever chosen and loved by your fiancée, you were chosen and loved by God. Being chosen and loved by God can make all the difference in the world in how you choose to love your new husband or wife. To give your marriage the strongest foundation possible and to dress your heart with the character qualities that no great marriage can do without, it's vital for you to understand that you are chosen and cherished and loved first by God. He's the one who created marriage, and He has all the strength and power to show you how to make your marriage work. With God, you can have your wedding cake and eat it too, but that doesn't mean He's going to do your wedding work for you. Like a tasty wedding cake, a great marriage is made by hard work and good choices. God supplies the wisdom, and we make the choices.

To make your marriage work in today's world, the first, oldest, and very best wedding wisdom available is choosing God to be the key influence on whatever you cook up in your marriage. When you know and accept God's love through Jesus Christ, you become a whole person. When you accept God's love and the sacrifice Christ made on your behalf, you'll receive what you need to make the inevitable sacrifices that are required to make a marriage great. When you know you're loved and chosen by God, you have all of His holiness, compassion, kindness, humility, gentleness, patience, support, forgiveness, love, and unity to make your marriage made in heaven work here on Planet Earth.

Every day of your marriage is a choice, and you've got a countless number of choices to make in the months and years ahead. By now, you're making (or have already made) a ton of wedding choices, but don't forget about the most important choice of all: You're choosing to love, and you're choosing to be chosen. You'll do plenty of packing for your honeymoon, but choosing to love and choosing to be chosen are what you want to be sure to pack in your heart as you start your new life together. Being chosen and loved by God is the very best wedding gift you could ever hope to receive, and it's the very best wedding gift you could ever give to the one you love! It's absolutely free, and you won't be working weekends to pay it off!

FOR NEARLYWEDS

How did you and your fiancée choose one another? What makes it so exciting to be chosen and loved by someone else? How is being in love different than choosing to love? In what ways will you be challenged to choose one another again and again throughout the course of your lives?

FOR NEWLYWEDS

How do your choices determine the success of your marriage? What are some good choices you've made so far in how you love and relate to one another? What are some poor choices you've made, and what can you learn from them? How can God's love give you the strength to choose each other every day?

Guys Are Prodigious Wedding Planners

6

What's the difference between a boyfriend and a husband? About thirty pounds.

—Cindy Garner

Who says guys don't do wedding planning? This simply isn't true. Guys are prodigious wedding planners, but not in the traditional sense of the word. Guys do a whole lot more planning and preparing for married life than they get credit for. Now that I think about it, guys are completely overlooked and, dare I say, underappreciated when it comes to matrimonial matters.

You can't plan a wedding if a guy doesn't plan the engagement.

But are guys ever recognized for outstanding engagement planning? Nobody ever says to a guy, "Hey, great job! That was the best wedding proposal I've ever seen! You really went all out washing your car like that! And the way you got down on your knee, *oouu-wee*, now that was tops! Who woulda ever thought of that? You must have spent months practicing those knee bends!"

I mean, who ever actually witnesses an engagement?

Witnessing an engagement is as rare as an inexpensive wedding. Engagements are solitary affairs. Friends and family aren't invited.

Nobody goes to an engagement.

No people. No praise.

Guys pour their life savings into a very special romantic evening and a big rock shipped all the way from a remote diamond mine in Africa. They expend enormous amounts of emotional energy on popping the Big Question, but what people never see is that most guys are so nervous getting ready for the engagement that they need a couple of buddies to hold 'em down and shave 'em out of fear of slicing off their face with a Bic razor and bleeding to death before they ever get a foot out the door. Shouldn't that count for something?

For *p-pop-popping-th-tha-ba-big-qwa-question*, guys barely get a golf clap.

To which women respond, "This is good. Humility is a very good thing."

Though women do the majority of planning for the actual wedding and reception, this is due to the fact that most women have been planning their weddings since the second grade. Deprive a woman of her wedding-planning dreams, and you're gonna go nose to nose with her inner child.

Engagement is merely a sideshow on the way to the big tent for the main event.

Guys run the sideshow. Women run the main event.

Sure, we guys don't have to deal with the more difficult decisions of wedding planning like choosing a cathedral train or swan butter knives or embossed invitations or flowered duvets or sprigs of spotted calla lilies versus brilliant pink tree peonies on the pews or flower-girl dresses or tiaras or toasting goblets or gift registries or Jordan almonds, which, when stale, have an absolutely hideous, chalky taste. (If a guest chokes on one of those pink puppies during your wedding reception, you'd better get yourself a good lawyer. Given our litigious society, I'd have every guest sign a "Chalky Jordan Almond Choking Waiver" before they set foot inside your reception. You never know what kinds of bottom dwellers exist on your future in-laws' side of the family.)

After the wedding proposal, guys are relegated to the obscure, behind-the-scenes duties that have to happen before the knot is tied, lest that knot be tied into a lynching noose and roped around their necks. One of the most common tasks a guy has to complete before the wedding is to clean out his apartment and to get it ready for future double occupancy.

This is where the song "Here Comes the Bride" is properly understood as a wedding march. Despite what many assume, "Here Comes the Bride" is not just a wedding song. It's a carry-the-bride-across-the-threshold air-raid siren warning that the groom's place had better be cleaner than a boot camp military barrack before the bride moves in.

Cleaning out the apartment in order to make it suitable for married life is one of the most pivotal, unsung tasks a guy undertakes to prepare for married life. While his fiancée is picking out bridesmaids' gifts and laboring over lacy ring pillow decisions, a guy can spend up to six months cleaning up and clearing out his apartment to make sure it passes marriage muster.

I want to cut that time in half.

Guys, consider this wedding-planning wisdom my bachelor gift to you.

Knowledge is power.

There are two simple steps for apartment cleaning that every groom has to do before his bride will ever consider setting foot into the door, let alone walking down the aisle with him. Call it grooming the groom's apartment. Or you can call it what it really is: a Hazmat toxic-waste dump cleanup.

The bachelor's pad must undergo a radical transformation.

The rat's nest must become a love nest.

The first step to apartment cleaning is a simple process called *stripping*. No, this has nothing to do with any bachelor-party fantasies you may entertain. Stripping is the process whereby you strip yourself of all earthly possessions that have anything to do with your former life as a bachelor. It's kind of like renouncing all your possessions when you join a religious cult that worships yak entrails or shaving your head when you become a Buddhist in order to enter the temple. Stripping is similar to these practices, but different. Most bachelors don't know the difference between yak entrails and Top Ramen.

As you might have suspected, stripping your apartment involves stripping the walls of your favorite *Charlie's Angels* posters. You also strip off the black-light poster of Rosie the Spanish flamenco dancer. You strip your entire bedroom of lava lamps, garage-sale furniture, autographed Richard Petty racecar posters, and the Etch A Sketch you had as a kid. Yes, say good-bye to Alfred E. Newman; your entire *Mad* magazine collection goes too. It's time to cash in the five-gallon Sparkletts water bottle half-filled with change. The proceeds will be used to purchase potpourri-scented clothes hangers for your former closet.

Once you strip your bedroom clean, you move into the TV room, where you strip that foul, despicable, moth-eaten Mexican blanket covered in smelly dog hair off the couch. You get rid of that ugly burlwood table whose sole use was for depositing pizza scraps and empty cans. Next, you move into the kitchen and begin to strip the . . .

Wait, I'm sorry. I'm going so hard on you here. This is tough on you, I know.

This job is too much for one guy. You've got enough on your mind as it is.

The kitchen alone will take weeks to clean. Who knows when it was cleaned last?

I've got an idea. Before you start stripping, I suggest you don't attempt these three serious apartment-cleaning steps alone. Much grief is involved. There are professional counselors trained to help engaged guys with this sort of problem. If a professional counselor isn't available, you may want to call Vinnie the garbage man because he's handled lots of bachelor crises like this before. On any given day, Vinnie only finishes half of his neighborhood trash route because he spends so much time consoling engaged guys who can't bear the thought of depositing entire collections of valuable guy stuff in a slimy dumpster: Old baseball caps. Sports equipment. Ten years' worth of *Sports Illustrated* swimsuit editions. *Freedom Rock* CDs purchased from infomercials. The losses are staggering. You may even need to put this book down and call Vinnie this very instant. You're gonna need to dump on him in more ways than one. If you're already married, Vinnie could sure use some help manning his 1-800-GUY-JUNK hotline. Vinnie's looking for a few good men to help you where it hurts. These guys know where you're coming from.

Once you're finished stripping your apartment and making your sacrificial marriage offering to the waste-disposal jaws of Vinnie's garbage gods, Vinnie will take off and make enough money for next summer's vacation in the Hamptons by putting all your beloved treasure on the lucrative bachelor black market.

After stripping, the second step in apartment cleaning is *sterilization.*

Take that frightened look off your face. *I'm not holding a knife.*

Your vasectomy is years away.

Sterilization is a biologically necessary step in order to bring your apartment up to standard health-and-safety code requirements. You've kept the Department of Health and Human Services at bay for long enough. If you don't sterilize your apartment, your new bride will report you to the authorities, and that is no way to start a life of wedded wonder.

Sterilization involves three separate spray treatments designed to rid the apartment of any nonhuman life forms, including but not limited to germ spores, refrigerator fungus, black mold in the shower, wart viruses in the carpet, malarial mosquitoes, and the boa constrictor that slithered into the closet last year and hasn't been seen since.

The first spray treatment in the sterilization process is the use of a high-powered, hand-held steam cleaner roughly the size of a fire hose. To sufficiently kill all life forms, you must exert great care in using the pressurized steam cleaner, lest you inadvertently vaporize yourself in the process. Many a bachelor has arrived at the altar wrapped in burn-ward bandages as a direct result of not paying attention to steam-cleaner warning labels and stealth boa constrictors going for the kill from overhead curtain rods.

The second spray treatment in the sterilization process is flea spray.

"What's a few fleas?" you exclaim.

Few is a relative term, and the few fleas that you've become very familiar and comfortable with have laid approximately sixty million tiny flea eggs in strategic locations throughout your apartment. Call it a bachelor flea prank, but despite what some entomologists may say, fleas do have a sense of humor. Should you fail to spray for this imminent infestation, your future bride is going to swell up to the size of the Hindenburg when she's attacked by the offspring of the same fleas you now consider to be familiar friends. Flea bites do not constitute a blood test as required by the state, but should you fail to ignite a flea bomb in your apartment, the fleas will gladly perform their own blood test on your new bride.

The third and final spray treatment in the sterilization process is cockroach spray.

This spray treatment, I do admit, is both dangerous and gruesome. Though animal activists will protest that cockroaches are people too, the cockroaches must die. Because you know that brides and cockroaches cannot peacefully coexist, you must diligently prepare for a cockroach revolution on a scale seldom seen before.

Most brides aren't aware that cockroaches have a shared-living agreement with most bachelors. In exchange for room and board, a group of guy cockroaches, known in their scientific grouping as a "huddle," cook the meals, do the cleaning, scour the kitchen plates, and take out the trash. When a guy's fiancée isn't around, the "huddle" doesn't worry about ducking under the refrigerator to escape the wrath of swatting broom. A huddle of cockroaches has a shared-living arrangement (usually in writing) with the same basic privileges as a human roommate who pays his rent in full every month. The huddle thinks, *We got rights, ya know. We cook. We clean. If the human guys in this place can sit around, eat popcorn, and watch Monday Night Football, there's no reason why we can't sit in the popcorn bowl, eat our share, and root for our favorite team too!* On a rotating basis, members of the cockroach huddle may be invited to jump into a few rounds of poker if one of the humans fails to show up, but this doesn't happen often because cockroaches are amazing card sharks. Their poker faces have won them plenty of jackpots.

Frankly, how you evict a huddle of cockroaches is beyond me. You better plan to spray for them, but they won't go easy. If you don't get 'em out before your wedding day, I wouldn't put it past them to rig some sort of elaborate foot-tripping, booby-trap device to launch you and your new bride across the steam-cleaned threshold. After you dump her on the ground, your wife will think you're psychotic if you start blaming a huddle of cockroaches for your clumsiness. You'll hear the cockroaches giving each other antennae-clicking high-fives as they laugh at you from under your new pink-flowered couch.

You have turned friends into enemies, and in their eyes, you're the traitor.

The cockroach wars have just begun.

TOGETHER FOREVER

You've got your whole lifetime to be married, but you and your future spouse get only one shot to make your wedding day one of the most special days of your lives. Your wedding day is a day you'll never want to forget. You want a perfect start to a perfect life together. What couple *doesn't* dream of the perfect start?

How many wedding receiving lines have you stood in where the newlyweds greeted you with gallows humor: "Bad day, isn't it? Ever seen a wedding as bad as ours? Go ahead and try the teriyaki chicken fingers . . . they're loaded with salmonella. Have a terrible day on us."

Nobody thinks like that. Nobody plans for a bad wedding day.

The day you got engaged, you knew, maybe almost expected, that there would be a number of jumps, bumps, and thumps getting ready for a wedding. You knew that a wedding engagement is an intense, emotional period with tons to do within a short amount of time. Three months. Six months. Maybe twelve months or the luxury of eighteen months to plan for a one-day celebration that makes a golden anniversary seem a millennium away. No matter how much time you have, the closer you get to the Big Day, there still never seems to be enough time. Especially when your cell phone rings minutes before the wedding, and you discover that your best man is being held at gunpoint by a huddle of angry, homeless cockroaches.

Some things you just can't plan for.

Who talks about planning for the perfect marriage? Because weddings are deadline driven, the wedding date becomes the center of your universe. The only deadline driving marriage is "till death do us part," which is something most people don't like to think about. Most people don't give much thought to marriage planning. They think that their marriage will live on love alone; besides, there's so much to get done for the wedding. Marriage, in comparison to engagement, doesn't have the pressing urgency of pulling off a wedding. Marriage seems to require less forethought and less planning because it's not a major one-day event, but a lifelong relationship. Marriage won't make you lie awake at 2:00 A.M. worrying if your caterer is capable of feeding hundreds of guests, but a wedding will.

"What's to plan?" you ask. "We love each other. We thought long and hard about this decision. Our choice is made. We're ready to grow old together watching the paint peel on the front porch. Our planning is over."

If you want to have a great marriage, and I'm sure you do, your planning is just beginning. Great weddings don't happen on accident, and neither do great marriages. Planning a wedding brings you together at the altar, but wedding planning does not guarantee you'll stay together forever. Marriage planning is not just something you do in a few, short premarital counseling sessions. Marriage planning is the determination and daily commitment to make your marriage succeed. To do whatever it takes to pull it off. Every day. For the rest of your life.

You pulled off your wedding. Now it's time to pull off your marriage.

So far, you've been a prodigious wedding planner, but the day will soon come when you need to be a prodigious marriage planner. I'm not talking about being a Type A person who schedules every meal, prepares budget spreadsheets for the next three years, times the conception and delivery of each child, and maps out every ride you take on a bicycle built for two. All I'm saying is that to make a marriage work, you have to be intentional and purposeful. And that requires some degree of planning in a way that works for you and your new spouse.

Have you heard the phrase "Aim at nothing, and you'll hit it every time?" You and your new spouse will get out of your marriage exactly what you put into it. Having your wedding cake and eating it too means you can't live on the rarefied air of pure love alone. Your wedding took a lot of work; can you expect anything different from your marriage? What goals do you have for your marriage? What dreams do you hope to accomplish over the course of your lifetime together? If you were to sketch out your ideal marriage, what would it look like? What would it take for you and your fiancée to create a together-forever kind of love? What will it take to put into practice the together-forever qualities of being chosen, holiness, compassion, kindness, humility, gentleness, patience, support, forgiveness, love, and unity? That's a tall order for creating an intimate, loving marriage. The only way to do it is by committing in your heart and mind that you will intentionally plan to make these qualities the form and substance of your life together.

Being a marriage planner means you and your spouse have to sit down on a regular basis to talk about your marriage—how you think it's going, which areas are going well, which areas need some extra work, and what you need from each other. Plan out fun dates, vacations, and retreats; settle any unresolved conflicts; and fess up to whoever ate the last pint of Starbucks mocha-chip ice cream in the fridge. Heck, top off your marriage planning with a wild time of making raucous love.

All work and no play makes Jack and Jill one dull couple.

To stay in good physical shape, you have to work out and watch how much ice cream you eat. Marriage is the same way. To keep your marriage from getting flabby, you have to do those things that keep your marriage healthy and alive. As you get busy with building your careers, raising a family, and taking on more responsibilities, you'll discover that life and marriage do not get simpler. Life gets more complicated, and your marriage is one of the easiest things to put on the back burner. If you invest your best time and energy into being intentional about your marriage, you'll discover that it's completely within your reach to have your wedding cake and eat it too.

No one plans for a bad wedding day or a bad marriage, but that's where some marriages end up. What would happen if you both put the necessary time and energy into planning every day for a great marriage? What kind of difference would it make in your marriage? Planning a perfect wedding is well worth the effort and garners you all sorts of applause as you walk hand in hand down the aisle together, but making your marriage a success is the applause you give one another when you see what a little marriage planning produces.

FOR NEARLYWEDS

Ask yourselves, "How much time do we spend talking about wedding plans versus marriage plans?" Both are important, but in perspective, your wedding is a one-day celebration, and your marriage is a lifelong commitment of love to one another. What type of planning do you think it takes to make a marriage succeed?

FOR NEWLYWEDS

Ask each other, "Right now, where would our marriage benefit the most by a little planning?" What will it take to accomplish your plans?

There Seems to Be a Slight Communication Problem

7

My wife says I never listen to her . . . or something like that.

The day before my wedding day, I made a dreadful discovery. No, it wasn't the altar apprehensions of whether Krista was the right one for me. And it wasn't the wake-up-sweating-and-screaming-in-the-middle-of-the-night realization that I'd forgotten to invite my aunt's best friend since second grade. My dreadful discovery wasn't that I'd failed to pick up my tux, nor was it finding out that my best man had lost the ring somewhere at the beach. Nor was it, woe of all dreadful discoveries, that my wedding day was actually *yesterday.*

My dreadful discovery was much simpler than that.

The day before my wedding day I discovered that there are two types of visas.

There is the credit-card visa. That's Visa with a capital *V*. This Visa is a passport to monthly-payment pain, a sort of financial Venus flytrap used by some couples to pay for their entire wedding by no later than their tenth wedding anniversary.

The second type of *visa,* which is the kind Krista and I needed, is a passport to physical pain. The kind of excruciating physical pain I experienced like a circus contortionist crammed in the back of Krista's tiny Honda CRX on the way home from the French consulate for three hours' worth of Los Angeles rush-hour traffic.

This second visa with a little *v* is the kind of visa that my travel agent failed to tell me I would need with our passports for our honeymoon to Europe. It is, according to Webster, the "official authorization stamped on a passport that permits entry into and travel within a particular country or region."

Like most communication problems, my communication problem with my travel agent began with a simple miscommunication. The night before the day before our wedding was our wedding rehearsal, in which Krista and I practiced learning how to walk like poised British royalty and how to stand without fainting (knees slightly bent like an NFL linebacker but a little more erect than a wax museum dummy). At the church, my buddies and I went easy on the wedding coordinator, and I was grateful none of us made her cry.

Later, we celebrated a wonderful rehearsal dinner at my folks' home with the wedding party, our families, and our friends. Lots of laughter, great food, toasts, and roasts made the perfect start for our prelaunch wedding-day countdown. All the wedding details were taken care of. Friday was wide open. There was nothing left to do.

Except pick up our airline tickets from the travel agent.

Krista and I drove to the travel agency, where our travel agent's assistant handed us our tickets and said, "Debbie's not here right now, but she wanted me to remind you that France is requiring visas for all American citizens. You'll have to pick them up before your flight leaves Monday morning."

Ever the prepared American tourist, I whipped out my wallet and pulled out my plastic. "I have a Visa."

"No, Mr. O'Connor. You need a visa with a little *v*, which is the official authorization stamped on a passport that permits entry into and travel within a particular country or region."

"Oh, that kind of visa. A visa with a little *v!* How nice of Debbie to drop this little reminder on us the day before our wedding."

I made a quick mental calculation: *Today is Friday. Foreign consulates are closed on weekends. We leave early Monday morning for France.*

"Excuse me, miss. Let me see if I understand you correctly. We reserved these plane tickets two months ago. Our wedding is tomorrow. We leave Monday morning, and you're just telling me now that we need 'a visa with a little *v*' to get into France. Am I missing anything here?"

"*C'est vrai!* You have to go to the French consulate *immediatemonte* and get your visas!"

The assistant was very polite. Debbie's slight communication problem was going to put a minor dent the size of Notre Dame into our honeymoon plans, but it wasn't her assistant's fault. But as I stood in front of the assistant emitting bad visa vibes, I had a new appreciation for the role of scapegoats, sacrificial lambs, and fall guys. Could this be why the roiling anger surging in my blood looked like the Allied invasion of Normandy? The rest of our conversation went something like this . . .

"I have an idea. My fiancée and I are getting married tomorrow. For our wedding gift, why doesn't Debbie go to the French Consulate and get our visas for us?"

"Well, Mr. O'Connor, Debbie's not here, and you have to apply for your visas in person. But you don't have to go to France, if you don't want to. However, your airline tickets are nonrefundable, and it's too late to change your departure date. Would you be interested in spending your honeymoon someplace else? I'm sure I can come up with something. Let me just check my computer here . . . oh, Hawaii's all booked up. Nothing's available in Mexico. Tahiti's long gone, and at this time of year you can forget the Caribbean and the Bahamas. I'll have to get you something a little closer to home, but I'll be saving you a lot of money."

Oh joy.

"There's a tractor-pull competition in Barstow that I'm sure your wife would love to attend. Or, I have a cozy little Buttonwillow bed and breakfast right next to the largest cattle slaughterhouse in the United States. A free tour of the slaughterhouse comes with every two-night stay. They even have free samples of *le boeuf*, ha-ha! Ahem, here I have the Twenty-Third Annual Rodent Roundup at the Bermuda Dunes trailer park, which is just outside Area 51 near Las Vegas. Residents of the trailer park say that several of their prized rodents have been abducted by space aliens just outside Area 51. This is the only trailer park with an official Alien Rodent Abduction Museum, but the government vehemently denies all rodent abduction allegations. They blame the rat disappearances on cats. A likely story."

Visiting a museum dedicated to the rat race in outer space was not the honeymoon in Vegas I had in mind. Months earlier, I formulated a very clear mental picture of what our European honeymoon was supposed to look and feel like. No rats. No cats. No aliens or trailer-park mysteries of the universe. My travel agent's assistant couldn't comprehend the emotional investment, let alone the financial investment, I had made for this trip.

"Excuse me, miss. I am not going to honeymoon with big rigs in Barstow, beef carcasses in Buttonwillow, or alien-abducted rats in the Bermuda Dunes trailer park. I am going to Paris, *The City of Love,* for my honeymoon. When my bride and I arrive in Paris, I will passionately kiss her on the Eiffel Tower. Krista and I will walk hand in hand down the Champs Élysées without getting held up. We will eat our *petit déjeuner* of French baguettes and *café au laits* at twenty dollars a pop. We will be lost in love at the Louvre, where we will look at the Mona Lisa and see our reflections in the plastic covering Mona Lisa's face. We will stare at French impressionist paintings and say, "Ooohh," as if we really understood the deeper existential philosophy of spilled paint on canvas. We will kneel at Napoleon's grave and then wonder what we're doing kneeling at Napoleon's grave. We will stroll through the gardens and palace of Versailles and make a bold swap for our eight-hundred-square-foot condo. And when the moon is bright and the feeling's right, we will make out like French lovers along the Seine River! Do I make myself perfectly clear?"

"*Oui, monsieur.*"

"Fine! Now please tell me where the French Consulate is in Orange County."

"There is no French Consulate in Orange County. You have to go all the way to Los Angeles. Depending on today's traffic, you might miss your wedding tomorrow. Call me if you change your mind about Bermuda Dunes. Have a great life."

Rather than dig in for trench warfare to fight a losing communication battle, Krista, my best man Tom, and I hopped into Krista's Honda and hightailed it up to the French Consulate near Beverly Hills. We waited in line for a couple of hours and finally got our visas with a little *v*. Since we were right next to Beverly Hills and this was the French Consulate, I was a bit disappointed there wasn't a French chef handing out escargot samples, brie, and French wine to those of us in line. We were going over to their country to spend our American dollars to help their economy. They could at least give us a few frog legs.

We left the consulate at 3:00 P.M., just in time to hit the notorious Los Angeles Friday afternoon bumper-to-bumper traffic. Krista's CRX was a little two-seater, so I squeezed into the hatchback area and sat like a lump of laundry thrown in the back. It wasn't too bad on the drive up, because that only took about forty-five minutes. But when your body is folded into human origami for three hours of starting and stopping, bumping and thumping like a human bowling ball getting knocked around in traffic, you can forget about any wedding-night gymnastics.

Trust me, this is not how you want to spend the day before your wedding.

I felt a new compassion for people who get smuggled into this country.

When we arrived at my place at 6:00 P.M., I crawled out of the car feeling as if someone had thrown me into a burlap bag and beat me with heavy bamboo sticks. My bum felt like someone shot me with a gallon of Novocain, and I wasn't sure if I'd ever be able to straighten my arms again. My neck was kinked like I was trying to look at the world upside down, and I wasn't sure if Krista would be willing to push my wheelchair for the rest of her life.

TOGETHER FOREVER

As you begin your prelaunch wedding-day countdown and enter into married life, you can count on plenty of slight and not-so-slight communication problems. Whether you're dealing with travel agents, photographers, videographers, caterers, wedding coordinators, seamstresses, in-laws, stepparents, friends, family members, or anyone else remotely involved in your Big Day, don't let communication problems suck you dry of what's most important for you and your fiancée. If you're not careful, a communication problem that began with a vendor or family member can come between you and your future spouse.

You only have so much time and energy to plan your wedding, so you need to decide where your best time and energy will be spent. Don't let your best creativity, enthusiasm, and energy get drained from a miscommunication that you now have no control over. If you have to drive to LA for visas with a little *v*, then drive to LA!

On our wedding day, Krista and I faced about the worst, worst-case wedding reception scenario possible. During our engagement, Krista had a number of very specific, face-to-face communications with our caterer. Two hundred or so guests were planning to attend the reception, so naturally we expected the caterer to do what caterers are supposed to do: feed our hungry guests. It wasn't French cuisine, but we weren't exactly serving Froot Loops either.

The caterer was in charge of having the correct amount of food to feed our guests. That was the first slight communication problem. About half our guests were served food on plates. The second half were served air on plates.

Lite fare. Lo-cal. Fat-free.

The second communication problem seemed to be about how to cook roast beef. Most people don't like roast beef that has the same body temperature of a freshly slaughtered steer. I'd even venture to say that most people don't eat *uncooked, blood-red roast beef*, but that's what they were served on our wedding day! There was a huge hunk of Buttonwillow beef sitting on the carving table that looked like it was fresh out of the slaughterhouse. The chef (who definitely was not French) was depositing whole hunks of inedible red meat into a trash can under the table. In the background, the DJ kept playing "Rawhide." Over and over and over . . .

"Rollin', rollin', rollin', keep dem doggies rollin', RAW-HIDE!"

"How do you like your meat, sir?"

"Dead and red. Hey, pour some of that French au jus on there . . . or is that blood?"

"Excuse me, but is that meat paid for or what? Do we get a refund for every pound you dump in the trash? And what about that salad? Do we each get a single shred of lettuce?"

At my wedding reception, I had an egg roll, a Diet Coke, and a slice of wedding cake. I was lucky to get seconds on the wedding cake because the rest of our guests were starving! Why didn't we think to order pizza?

Krista was mortified. My father-in-law paid for food that was thrown in the trash, and our wedding banquet turned into a Food for the Hungry rally. It was too late to scrounge two-for-one coupons for Big Macs at McDonald's, so what could we do?

We had a great time. We danced. We had our wedding cake and ate it too. Our wedding day was one of the best days of our lives.

Throughout all the details of your wedding planning and into your married life, you'll find real wisdom in choosing your battles wisely. Some communication problems aren't worth fighting about, especially if a third party is coming between you and your spouse. When money's on the line or you're worried about what other people will think about your wedding day, it's really easy to assert that you're right, to dig into your defenses, and to develop a battle plan for trench warfare.

But at what cost?

Arguing over agapanthuses versus antherium just isn't worth it sometimes. Of course, some principles and situations are worth fighting for, especially when someone is trying to take you to the cleaners, but you and your spouse would be wise to talk about which battles are worth fighting over together and which battles aren't worth a salad spinner.

In this life and in your marriage, there are always going to be slight miscommunications, major "How-did-we-miss-this?" misfires, and flagrant misunderstandings. Just as you can expect to have a number of miscommunications in planning a wedding, you can expect marriage to have its fair share of well-intended communications that go awry. But marriage is also the great place where you get to communicate a lot of wonderful words and meaningful messages to your new spouse.

"Good-bye! Have a great day!"

"I love you!"

"Wow! You look great in that new outfit."

"I really appreciate who you are."

"Thanks for helping do the dishes."

"You are the cream in my coffee."

As sugar-sweetened as those lovey-dovey words are, marriage is the place where words can arrive like a bouquet of flowers or like a brick through the front window in the middle of the night. If marriage didn't have communication problems, it wouldn't be marriage! That's why during your marriage preparations, you want to be sure to work on how you communicate with one another. To have your wedding cake and eat it too means you need to work on the necessary but often-overlooked skills of listening, seeking to understand your spouse's perspective, using words that build up and don't tear down, watching the tone of your voice, avoiding interrupting, and speaking to your spouse in the same considerate way you'd like to be spoken to. Too often, slight communication problems erupt into full-blown communication conflicts because a husband and wife don't take the time to fully hear each other out. Working on being a good communicator is the way to wedded wonder, but it only happens when you each give your best efforts to understand your spouse.

Clear communication is the crucial link in developing a together-forever love between you and your spouse. Focus your time and energy on solving problems together. Don't allow others to come between you by allowing a slight communication problem to create major static in your relationship. Most of all, when you do have your differences (and you will!), don't let your differences keep you from forgiving one another and communicating your love for one another.

If you don't make a major beef over everything, you just might find some extra frog legs lying around.

FOR NEARLYWEDS

What slight communication problems have you had with vendors or relatives that have created problems between you and your fiancée? What helps you and your fiancée resolve communication problems? How will learning effective ways to resolve communication conflicts now help you in your marriage later?

FOR NEWLYWEDS

In which areas of your relationship do you have good communication? In which areas do you most often have communication conflicts? Name one communication skill that would make the most difference in your relationship. What can you do to work on that skill today?

The Money Dance Is Not the Chicken Dance

8

Marriage is Wall Street's most overlooked merger and acquisition. No other investment can send you skyrocketing and plummeting so many times in the same day.

At my wedding reception, I missed the financial opportunity of a lifetime, and I'm still paying for it. When, tell me, are people ever again going to pay me money for the chance to dance with my wife? I could have bankrolled our whole honeymoon tax-free by setting up shop on the dance floor. But nooooo, I was too busy dancing to the California Grape song, swooning away like a wrinkled raisin to lyrics I'd heard a million times before: "Ooooh, I heard it on the grapevine."

Yeah, let's talk sour grapes.

The money dance is a cash crop, and I missed out big time.

Who needs a honeymoon in Vegas when the money-dance odds are one hundred to one in your favor?

When I got married, I didn't even know what the money dance was. That's just one of many gripes I have with my premarital counselor. He certainly wasn't a financial counselor, that's for sure. I want to know how come nobody told me that this was my chance to make back all the money I spent on her diamond ring and then some?

When I was a kid, I saw the money dance maybe one or two times, but I had no idea what it was. For free cake and a glass of stolen champagne, weddings were about the only events worth getting dressed up for as a kid. All I saw on the dance floor was the bride with a flimsy Cinderella-type purse attached to her wrist like a Jacques Cousteau divebag. Older men would walk up to the bride, slip something into it, and bump the slop she was dancing with out of the picture. How'd I know what they were putting in the bag? I thought it was something like the bait they give to dolphins after they do a really cool flip at Sea World or one of those mackerel they give to Shamu for licking naive tourists from Saskatchewan with his huge pink tongue when what Shamu really wants to do is open that humongous mouth of his, swallow them up to their bellybuttons, flip 'em off the platform, and finish 'em off like fish chum at the bottom of the pool. Now that's a killer whale show!

I thought the stuff going into the divebag was anchovies. Fish heads. Kippers.

Nobody ever told me it was money!

As a kid, I knew nothing about marriage or weddings or lining a purse with so much cash you need a Brinks truck and armed guards to haul it away. What did I know about paying bills, saving some for a rainy day, and postwedding credit-card debt? For all I knew, the money dance was the same thing as the chicken dance. I thought that's why environmentalists wanted people to throw birdseed instead of rice at the bride and groom. At my wedding, all I did was the funky chicken, and to this day, I have nothing to show for it.

If I only knew then what I know now, I would be experiencing all the financial freedom in the world like those Hawaiian tourists sitting in directors' chairs in Waikiki on late-night real-estate infomercials. I could have starred in one of those infomercials . . .

That's right, Herb, last I checked, my net worth has skyrocketed to more than four million dollars. The money dance gave my wife and me the ten thousand dollars we needed to make deposits on three foreclosure properties for NO MONEY DOWN! We now own three hundred rental units, eight trailer parks, minus seven that were destroyed by twisters in seven separate states, and three rat-infested buildings, but we don't talk about those. This business is so simple, you could give me a lobotomy, and I'd still be making money hand over fist. I owe everything I have to the money dance.

I could've been a contender.

I could've been The Donald.

Guys, if you haven't gotten married yet, I'm going to bankroll your financial future with the following advice: If you married for love and not money, the money dance is your last chance to fill the deficit in your savings account. If you're newly married, like me, you missed the opportunity of a lifetime, but don't worry. You can come and work with me at KFC on the weekends. The chicken's tasty, but the grease is a killer on the pores.

The money dance is the only legitimate and legal way of charging others for services rendered by your wife. This is a simple business arrangement that has enormous financial ramifications. Your job is to rent out your wife for a minute or so. I don't care if she waltzes, boogie-woogies, or slam dances in a mosh pit. All she has to do is dance.

Wait.

Okay, I do agree with you on that one.

The lambada is off-limits.

Now that I think of it, there are a number of songs that you can't pick for the money dance. You really don't know your in-laws that well yet, so I suggest you also avoid playing the following songs. You do want to get invited over for Christmas dinner.

THE TOP TEN SONGS NOT TO PLAY AT YOUR WEDDING

1. "A Boy Named Sue"
2. "Yo Yo Big Daddy, Your Baby's All Mine Now"

3. "She's Got Legs" (or any song by ZZ Top)
4. "To All the Girls I've Loved Before"
5. Sousa's "Shotgun Wedding March"
6. "Love Stinks"
7. *The Addams Family* theme song
8. "Dueling Banjos" from the movie *Deliverance*
9. "She's a Brick House"
10. Mozart's *Requiem*

The first thing you need to do is completely redo your wedding-invitation list. You bride-to-be may protest at first, but once you run the numbers and show her the bottom line, she'll think you're a financial genius. The only women your bride gets to invite to the wedding are her mother, sisters, and bridesmaids. That's it. No more. Men want to dance with the bride. The money dance doesn't work any other way. Women who want to come up to hug and kiss the bride are a distraction. If a guy's gonna pay good money to dance with the bride, he wants to get his money's worth.

The focus of the wedding-invitation list, like the money dance, is money. The majority of the wedding invitation list is reserved for your father's friends and her father's friends of substantial wealth. Sorry, but that automatically excludes any of your buddies thirty and younger who are on the lower rungs of the corporate food chain. This means you gotta make sacrifices too. If you're going to maximize your money-dance profits, your dad has to be your best man. No college buddies. No former teammates. No childhood friends. You don't need any freeloading groomsmen, especially those who expect you to rent their tux just because they're flying all the way across the country to do for you what you did for them. Drop 'em. They're financial dead weight. If you do have a few buddies who insist on attending, they must first submit a "Wedding

Dance Pledge Card" and a copy of last year's tax return. So what if the wedding party looks lopsided at the altar and in the wedding photos; do you want nice pictures or a nice, fat bank account? You decide.

Once you've cleaned up your wedding-invitation list, include the following information in your actual wedding invitation. Again, your bride-to-be may protest, but tell her the choice is absolutely up to her if she wants to be married to a Waikiki real-estate magnet or if she wants to be fishing rats out of the deep fryer at KFC for the rest of her life. Here's what to include on your flyer:

Money Dance Lottery

At the wedding of ____ and ____, tickets for the Money Dance Lottery will be sold for one thousand dollars each. At the end of the reception, a ten-thousand-dollar prize will be given to the lucky winner.

All Major Credit Cards Accepted

This is a foolproof formula for money-dance financial success. All your dad's friends are used to being hit up for charity golf tournaments, church-building programs, and various philanthropic civic organizations. Your money dance lottery gives them a chance to dance with the bride and walk away with ten thousand dollars in cash. Talk about a great wedding! You can't miss with this one. Run the numbers yourself. If you invite, say, three hundred men to your wedding and only a hundred ante up for the money dance lottery, you shell out only ten grand for the prize, and you bank ninety grand! That's what I call making money with no money down.

Now, once your wedding reception starts, you'll need to have the dance floor fenced off to create an atmosphere of exclusivity similar to that of a Hollywood movie premiere. Security guards are optional, but you will need cordoned aisles to keep any troublemakers from cutting in line. Your bride's job is to dance until her feet fall off or until she passes out, whichever comes first. Your job is to man the table where you collect cash, checks, or charges for the various money dances the guys can participate in. I say "various" because your actual goal is to make the whole reception one big money dance. Remember, we're talking financial freedom. Don't settle for a few fish sticks in the divebag. You've got a captive audience, so grab a marlin gaffer and go for it.

I've heard that the following money dances really roll in the dough: the "She's-not-marrying-me-for-my-money" money dance, the "Didn't-your-parents-teach-you-money-doesn't-grow-on-trees?" money dance, the "Maybe-we-should-splurge-just-this-once" money dance, the "We-can't-afford-that!" money dance, and the "My-wife-has-a-degree-in-retail-therapy" money dance.

Save the lottery for last. Like Shamu, it ends the show with a huge splash.

You and your unconscious bride can hula your way to Waikiki real-estate magnetdom.

When you get an open weekend, c'mon in to KFC and visit me some time.

TOGETHER FOREVER

People have all sorts of strong feelings about the money dance. Some think that the money dance amounts to glorified begging by putting people on the spot to cough up cash just for a chance to dance with the bride. (These people are really closet socialists, but that's just my humble opinion.) The way I see it is that two guys (the groom and the bride's father) are coughing up all sorts of cash to get this woman married, so why shouldn't the other guys in attendance feel some financial pain in their lower walletus maximus if they want to dance with the bride? In cases like this, Rule #1 of this book is broken: Guys who want to dance with the bride can't have their cake and eat it too. The wedding cake is free, but a dance with the bride will cost them beaucoup bucks. If the bride is kicking in her own cash to help pay for the wedding, all the more reason for her to have a chance to recoup her investment.

In other cultures, people feel very strongly about the importance of the money dance. Had I known this before I was married, I might have been tempted to change my nationality. In a country like the Philippines, money is accepted and expected as a regular wedding ritual the same as a dowry is expected in Micronesia or Papua New Guinea. If I had my choice between a dugout canoe, eight baboons, twenty pigs, three pythons, eight spears, fifty gourds, and a lifetime supply of poi, I'd probably take the cash, but who knows? I just might acquire a taste for poi.

I don't know what your feelings are about the money dance. You may think it's tacky. You may think it's terrific. But one thing you can definitely count on when you get married is that you and your spouse will be dancing all sorts of dances throughout the course of married life. Now I'm almost positive nobody's told you about all these different types of marriage dances, but what makes this book such an invaluable resource is that I slice up and serve you a slice of married life for exactly what it is.

The money dance is just one of many marriage dances. There's also the "Turn-off-that-stupid-Arnold-Schwarzenegger-movie-and-talk-to-me" communication dance. There's the "My-wife-is-pregnant-and-nauseous-to-the-point-of-death" pregnancy dance. There's the "It's-your-turn-to-change-your-son" diaper dance. There's the "What-did-I-ever-do-to-make-your-mother-hate-me?" in-law dance. And we mustn't forget about the "Honey-it's-been-three-weeks-since-our-last-conjugal-visit" sex dance, which is vehemently countered with the "If-you-want-me-you-must-first-nurture- and -romance-me" emotional intimacy dance.

These are just a few of the different types of dances that make up married life, but one of the secrets to having your wedding cake and eating it too is making sure you stay in step with your dance partner.

Especially on money matters. After the wedding reception is over, you can count on doing the money dance with your spouse for the rest of your lives. People may have strong feelings about the money dance at weddings, but if you want to really see where people's strong feelings about money rise to the surface, just look at married life.

In your marriage, money is not a subject you want to dance around. You and your spouse enter marriage with individual beliefs, values, feelings, myths, experiences, and ideas about how money should be earned, spent, saved, or given away. Your view of money is largely influenced by your parents and the family background in which these values were taught, shaped, and developed. You each have your own financial history, whether you have thousands stored in savings or thousands of dollars in credit-card debt. You could have a few dings on your credit record or a stellar balance sheet for all of your personal finances. You may have a solid employment track record, or you may change jobs as fast as an unemployed pool cleaner who likes to snowboard. You may have expensive taste and love to shop in the finest stores, or you may be as conservative and frugal as a Dutch banker from the Great Depression. Whatever your financial history may be, getting on the same balance sheet with your spouse is one of the best long-term investments you can ever make for your marriage.

The money dance is one of the most common areas for married couples to step on each other's toes. Money trouble and financial pressure can be a constant source of tension for nearly married, newlywed, and not-so-newlywed couples. Overdrawn bank accounts, credit-card debts, job losses, risky investments, tax audits, and overspending can lead to emotional bankruptcy in your marriage quicker than ATM usage fees. You can protect your most important earthly investment, your marriage, by working together to make your money work for you. Here are a few things to think about as you invest in each other's lives in the years to come.

Master Your Money. Some couples make money their master, so they spend their whole lives pursuing it, chasing it, and wanting more and more of it. Soon, it doesn't matter how much money they have or don't have because their money and their desire for more of it control practically everything they do. When you work at mastering your money together, your marriage wins.

To master your money, it's critical that you understand each other's thoughts, values, and beliefs about how money should be used in your marriage. By making money your servant, you get to control it instead of being mastered by it. During the next few years, you are going to make all sorts of important decisions about how to use your money: whether you should rent or buy a home, what kind of cars to own or lease, what types of investments to make, where to put your money to use if you get a big raise or inheritance, when to start a college fund for your kids, and when to start saving for retirement. The financial checklist goes on and on. By developing a shared financial philosophy and shared financial goals, you will be able to master your money instead of having the Almighty Dollar rule your marriage. Here's my two cents' worth: Couples who work at mastering their money are making a great investment for peace and harmony in their marriage. Be one of those couples.

Avoid Consumer Debt. Maybe you are already feeling pummeled by large credit-card debts. Nowadays, more and more couples are putting whole weddings and receptions on credit cards and leaving the financial chips to fall wherever they may fall once the wedding is over. If at all possible, don't be Visa's next victim. The first few months and years of marriage have enough change, stress, and pressure without adding additional financial pressure, so if at all possible, avoid putting more stress on your new marriage by heavy consumer debt. Pay off those credit-card balances as soon as you can. Once you do, you and your spouse will be free to master your money instead of getting nasty letters and fines from MasterCard.

A good question you might want to ask yourself is, "How important is it for me to be wealthy?" But there's another question that's probably more important: "How important is it for me to *look* wealthy?"

A lot of couples never take the time to ask themselves or each other these important questions, and the result is that they do the money dance on borrowed cash. Literally, play money. Abusing credit cards and lines of credit, they play Monopoly by creating an illusion of wealth. They *look* very wealthy tooling around town in expensive clothes, fancy cars, and lots of toys, but their net worth is negative because they're living on borrowed cash. They go for owning Boardwalk, but their creditors end up taking 'em to the cleaners. Make wise choices about consumer debt, and your marriage won't wind up in a financial straitjacket.

Raise the Standard of Your Marriage. Everyone wants to raise his or her standard of living. Don't believe it: Just listen to people talk about their Christmas lists in the middle of June. *I want the latest model car. A bigger home. A nicer neighborhood. New jewelry. A big-screen TV the size of Imax. An exciting adventure to study Papua New Guinean wedding rituals. I'm going to make a killing on a hot Internet IPO. I want more, more, MOOOORRRREEE. Big is better. Way better.*

Upsizing. It's the American way.

Nobody ever talks about raising the standard of marriage. But for all the time and energy spent earning a living, getting ahead, and hopefully blowing past the Joneses, what kind of difference will it ultimately make in your marriage?

You can raise the standard of your marriage by talking, listening, and working at mastering your money together. It takes a team effort to figure out who pays the bills, who searches for the best deals, who does the taxes, who earns the money, where the money is spent, and all the hundreds of decisions that lead your marriage off in the right financial direction, which is why I'm so glad I'm not a CPA, financial planner, or IRS agent.

When you think about it, though, we're all financial planners. The trick is being smart with what you've got. It doesn't matter if you come from a wealthy family or a poor family, whether you make a high salary or minimum wage, whether you won the money dance lottery or you just gave away your last nickel to dance with the bride: Every marriage has to dance the money dance. It's up to you whether you're going to get down and boogie your bucks in the right direction or whether you and your spouse are going to slam dance each other into financial oblivion. Your marriage is the best investment you could ever make, and it takes a delicate two-step to master your money together.

Once you figure out the money dance, you'll be ready to grab an accordion and do what every newlywed couple lives for! The chicken dance!

Na-na-na-na-na-na-na!

FOR NEARLYWEDS

Have you taken the time to talk about your attitudes and your use of money? How do you earn, save, spend, invest, and give your money away? Why is it really important to get a handle on your finances before you get married?

FOR NEWLYWEDS

In which areas are you good at handling your money together? In which areas do you need to work on how you use your money? How can sharing a similar perspective on financial management help eliminate money problems in your marriage?

Forces of Nature

9

Women will never be equal to men until they can walk down the street with a bald head and a beer gut and still think they are beautiful.

The morning after our honeymoon night, Krista and I talked about sex.

We also talked about how we could have chosen someone else to marry.

If you and I were to take a brief survey about which question newlyweds would prefer to discuss over a morning brunch of champagne and eggs Benedict, what do you think the politically correct newlywed response would be?

Sex! Definitely talk about the sex. Good or bad, be positive and talk about the sex.

Don't talk about marrying other people the day after your wedding!

Don't go there!

Now I suppose that a lot of people talk about sex on their honeymoon or prefer to spend a lot of time making love instead of talking about it, but I don't think many couples talk about all the other people they *could have married* when the person they chose *to marry* is sitting right across from them on the first day of their new lives together. That kind of awkward conversation conjures up all sorts of awful images of former boyfriends and girlfriends, doubts and insecurities about being a new husband or wife, or some sort of last resort salvation from the singles' scene. But that's exactly the conversation Krista and I had the morning after our wedding night.

After getting married in a blue country church in San Juan Capistrano and celebrating our reception at a beach clubhouse in Dana Point, Krista and I sped off to Palm Desert for the weekend. Our wedding night was a whole lot of fun, and the next morning we went to brunch at the Marriott hotel. With the bright sun shining on the Santa Rosa and San Jacinto Mountain peaks overlooking the land of golf courses, swimming pools, and palm trees, we couldn't have asked for a more beautiful desert morning.

As we ate our breakfast on a patio overlooking the immaculate hotel grounds, enjoying the warm morning sun, and drinking cup after cup of coffee, Krista and I talked about the wonderful, thoroughly pleasurable, yet temporary nature of sex. Some people have great wedding nights; others have terrible wedding nights. Regardless of how the wedding night goes, sex can be thrilling. Exciting. Passionate. Downright orgasmic.

And then it's over.

Yes, sex is great, one of the best gifts God's given to this world, but sex would be a real drag if you didn't like the person you married. As much as we enjoyed our wedding night, we knew there had to be so much more to marriage than sex for sex's sake. This sexy conversation and intimate ruminating led us to acknowledging the simple fact that we both could have married someone else. We could have married one of many other people.

If we'd looked long enough, we both could have found someone who was prettier, smarter, wealthier, wittier, or more handsome than either of us. There could have been *That Someone* who had something extra special to knock us off each other's romance radar screens.

Krista could have found someone who doesn't think disgusting spit tricks are funny. Krista definitely could have married someone wealthier than I was, which would have been just about anyone who didn't work for a church or fast-food burger joint. In the same way, instead of appreciating Krista just for who she was, I could have looked and looked to see if the grass was a little greener on the other side. Maybe that *Someone a Little Bit More Special* was just about to walk around the corner and change my life forever. Should I hold out just a little longer?

We have a tendency to think that way when we're single, don't we?

Some of us want to keep our options open for as long as possible.

The only problem is that before and after marriage, there are always more options.

Marriage is about making a choice and choosing to keep making the same choice.

Just the other day, Krista told me the story of dating a really cute guy in college. In her words, the guy was "total *GQ* material." The only problem was this guy had the personality of a doorknob and was more boring than the best shade of beige. In Krista's words, "Cute can only get you so far." I don't know this *GQ* guy's name, but to personalize our story, we'll call him "Boris."

What bored Krista the most about Boris was that he would explain things in minute detail on topics about which Krista was already well informed.

Why does he keep telling me things I already know?

Now remember that Boris is "total *GQ* material," so even though he was interesting to look at, whenever Boris spoke, Krista was tempted to feign a massive brain seizure to end the date right then and there. Given her many options, if Krista had wanted, she could have married Boris for his *GQ* looks and his designer genes. But if she'd married Boris, she would have had to relearn everything she already knew by the age of four.

For example, Krista and Boris are on a boring date walking up and down State Street in Santa Barbara, California. They pass by a shoe store, and Boris stops. He looks at Krista's feet.

"Krista, you're wearing sandals."

"Yes, Boris, these are leather sandals. Like shoes, they protect my feet from stepping on broken glass and other sharp objects."

"But they don't protect your toes. You could stub your toe if you're not careful. Have you ever thought about shoes with laces?"

Boris motions to Krista, and they walk inside the shoe store. Boris points.

"This is a shoe with laces."

"Boris, I have shoes with laces. I like sandals because they slip right on."

"Well, Krista, it doesn't take long to lace up a shoe."

Boris picks up the shoe with laces. *Real laces.*

"First, you make two bunny ears. You go over and under and follow the bunny into the hole and voilà, your laces are tied."

"Boris, I know how to tie my shoes."

Boris picks up another shoe.

"Now, Krista, if you don't like tying your shoes, you can always opt for one like this with the Velcro straps, but these are cheater-cheater-pumpkin-eater shoes."

When the totally *GQ* boring Boris called Krista a week later to go out on another date, Krista decided to give him a second chance. This time, though, she made it perfectly clear that she intended to wear sandals again.

On this boring date, Boris decides to get very creative by taking Krista out to dinner at a nice seafood restaurant on the Santa Barbara pier. Looking very snappy in his *GQ* polo shirt, crisp pleated pants, and leather loafers with no socks yet with full protective toe coverage, Boris is the perfect gentleman. Until he opens his mouth.

"Do you know why they call it seafood, Krista?"

Now as Krista knows, if it had been me sitting at the table, I would have unashamedly opened my mouth as wide as possible to impress her with my sourdough-roll seafood joke, "Zthee! Dis-iss-wha-thay-cal-id-seee-fuuud!"

But I'm not total *GQ* material, and I wasn't there.

So Krista responds to Boris. "Let me guess, Boris. It must be for a slightly different reason than they don't call cows, fruits, or vegetables *landfood*."

"Oh, you're close, Krista, but not close enough. The reason they call seafood *seafood* is because the fish on our plates come from the sea. It is *food* that comes from the *sea . . . seafood!* Isn't that amazing?"

Krista's eyes suddenly roll back in her head. She starts to shake and tremble.

"Krista! What's wrong?"

Krista falls to the floor, her body flopping up and down like a hooked halibut.

Boris panics, but his leather loafers with full protective toe coverage stay on as he drops to Krista's side.

"Help! Anybody! Is there a doctor in the house? I think my date's having some sort of seizure!"

TOGETHER FOREVER

As much as you and your spouse love one another, you could have married someone else. If Boris weren't so boring, Krista could be counting all the lace-up shoes in her closet right now. With me, she gets no grief about wearing sandals. If I wouldn't have had so many girlfriends break up with me in junior high and high school, I could be married to lots of women within the California State Penitentiary system.

Remember the movie *Forces of Nature*? After putting our four kiddos to bed the other night, Krista and I popped this flick into the VCR and snuggled next to each other on the couch. I thought I was in for another "romantic comedy" (which is just a movie industry term for "chick flick"), but the movie made a number of interesting observations about marriage and relationships.

Ben Affleck plays a likable guy named Ben, who's traveling from

New York to Georgia to get married. On his flight to Georgia, Ben meets a free spirit named Sara, played by Sandra Bullock. Sara's headed to Georgia to wrench her way out of a bad marriage and spend time with her six-year-old son, but when their plane crashes on takeoff and Ben rescues Sara, the "forces of nature" seem to pull them together in every imaginable situation. Ben is doing all he can do to get to his fiancée for his wedding day, but like the hurricane that keeps messing up his travel plans, Ben slowly gets sucked into the magnetism of Sara's seductive personality.

In this *Planes, Trains, and Automobiles* wedding spoof, Ben has plenty of opportunity to have sex with Sara, and all along we see him battling not only the hurricane that is keeping him from getting to his fiancée, but his sexual desires as well. What complicates Ben's perspective is that almost everyone Ben encounters has a terrible spin on marriage.

At his bachelor party, a beautiful flamenco dancer sends Ben's lust-seized grandpa into a near coronary. At the hospital, his grandpa secretly reveals that, after fifty years of marriage, he's never cared much for Ben's grandma. On the plane, Ben sits next to a guy who's grateful for his divorce and hated the marriage dilemmas of morning breath and sexual tension. In a car, Ben meets a guy who caught his wife in the shower with his brother. On a train, Ben and Sara meet a pleasant couple in their fifties who've never been happier in their lives . . . because of the splendid affair they're having. Ben gets his final rattle when he questions his own parents about their marriage: "Mom, Dad, are you happy?"

"Ben, that's not the point."

Dazed and confused, enamored with someone he met only two days earlier, and ready to chuck it all, Ben finally arrives late to his wedding while the hurricane rages. After battling the interior and exterior forces of nature throughout his journey, Ben now has to confront his fiancée who, unbeknownst to Ben, has been battling her own forces of nature with a former boyfriend.

As Sara waits in the rain for Ben to call off the wedding and watches as the hurricane destroys the wedding grounds, Ben's eyes look up to a balcony, where his bride is searching, waiting for him in the midst of the storm. Their eyes meet, and Ben's heart spills out this amazing revelation:

I always thought that there was one perfect person for everybody in this world. And when you found that person, the rest of the world just kind of magically faded away, and the two of you would be inside of this kind of protective bubble. But there is no protective bubble, or if there is, we have to make it. I think that life is more than a series of moments. We can make choices. We can choose to protect the people we love, and that's what makes us who we are, and those are the real miracles.

Ben could have chosen Sara.

Krista could have chosen Boris.

You could have chosen someone else.

We all could have chosen someone else . . . but we didn't.

We made our choice, and now we have the choice to protect the people we love.

For all the humor and laughter I love to put in my books, I also want to give you a gut check about the forces of nature that can sink your marriage if you're not careful. You can't have a great marriage if you aren't realistic about the forces of nature that can destroy your marriage. I would not be serving you, your spouse, or your marriage if we didn't have a frank talk about the power of our choices. The power for good or the power for bad. The choice to preserve or the choice to destroy. The choice to create a wonderful life together or the choice to shatter our own dreams. The choice to work through the tough times or the choice to throw in the towel.

I wish it were true, but marriage doesn't have any protective bubble.

We're given choices, and our choices are the best protection we have.

We come into marriage excited, enthusiastic, and eager to have our highest hopes and expectations met by our new spouse. But we also enter marriage as less-than-perfect people. I'd be foolish to tell you that your marriage can make it on your own power, because even the best marriages are tested to extremes. There is a power so great, so destructive, so terribly overwhelming that we don't really understand it. It's the power of sin. Call it selfishness, if you'd prefer. Sin or selfishness, like gravity, will pull you away from your marriage and one another because sin is always looking out for its own self-interest. Marriage is a "both/and" relationship. It is two "me's" that create a "we." You have needs, and your spouse has needs. Marriage is a constant balancing act of meeting each other's needs and serving one another in love. You take your needs *and* the needs of your spouse into consideration. Sin, however, takes only its own needs into consideration. Selfishness refuses to grow, change, flex, adapt, and do whatever it takes to make a marriage work.

We enter marriage as broken people who have strengths and talents and abilities that help us to be productive people, but we also have the fundamental flaws in our character that are always looking for an easy way out. No matter how much money we have, no matter how good we are, no matter what kind of job we have or how important we are, we are all broken by the force of sin in our lives. The good we want to do, we don't do, and the bad we don't want to do, we do. Yes, that's right, we doo-doo all the time. Marriage, for all the good it is, is also the messy place of a doo-doo here and a doo-doo there. You and your beloved just won't be able to avoid each other's doo-dooing.

The fundamental force of human nature that every husband and every wife has to reckon with in marriage is the powerful force of selfishness. Selfishness is nothing more than the self-centered force of sin in our lives. A lot of marriage books focus on understanding the differences between men and women, but they rarely talk about selfishness or the power of sin. Selfishness keeps you focused on your own needs first and your spouse's needs last. Left unchecked, selfishness will drive a huge wedge between you and your spouse. It would be a wonderful, yes, perfect world if your spouse could meet your every specific physical, emotional, intellectual, financial, social, and spiritual need, but no one person can meet all of your needs. Having all those needs makes you human, but it just isn't humanly possible for one person to meet your every need at the moment you'd like. That just wouldn't be a realistic picture of marriage.

When selfishness is getting the upper hand in your marriage, like Ben struggling with his doubts, it's easy to start believing everyone who has something negative to say about marriage. Don't listen to the antimarriage mongrels. Every marriage struggles with selfishness, and your marriage is no different.

You know what selfishness looks like. Watching television is one of the simplest ways to measure the selfishness symptoms in your marriage. She wants to watch something intelligent like *Masterpiece Theatre* or *Martha Stewart Living*. He wants to watch *Fifteen Days of James Bond* (which means fifteen days of Bond women) or the entire NCAA basketball championship plus replays. Who controls the remote becomes a major control issue. Selfishness explains why the average American household has four television sets.

Ask any married couple, and they will tell you (if they're honest) that even though you love your spouse, there will be times when you both act like rebellious, stubborn, impetuous children. You want to have your cake and eat it too, but in marriage, it's impossible to have your wedding cake and eat it too if you want everything or mostly everything your own way. Wedding cake is meant to be shared, and marriage is a daily agreement to share and share alike. The rules of the playground are the same. If you want to have a friend, be a friend. If you want others to share, then share. If you want to be loved, then love. If you want your needs to be met, be willing to meet your spouse's needs.

When you got married, you had very specific reasons why you chose to marry your spouse. It wasn't the forces of nature pulling you together. It was your mutual attraction for one another and, more importantly, your choices. The way some people explain "falling in love" today makes it sound like they had no personal responsibility or choice in the matter. It was "destiny" or "fate" or "planetary alignment" or the "blue-light specials on Aisle 4" that pulled them together. Loving someone, on this level of thinking, sounds vaguely familiar to falling into a huge gravel pit.

"We fell in love." *We fell in a pit.*

"We fell out of love." *We fell out of a pit.*

Selfishness has a sneaky way of explaining the forces of nature.

Loving someone does not happen by accident. Love is a choice. We choose either to love or not to love. What makes a marriage work is when you and your spouse keep choosing to love one another. Your love is defined by a specific choice demonstrated by a firm commitment to love your spouse through the inevitable ups and downs, twists and turns, mountains and valleys, conflicts and problems, frustrations and tensions that are a part of every marriage.

Fortunately, the Bible doesn't give us the bad news about sin and selfishness without giving us the good news too. The forces of your selfish nature don't have to rule in your life or ruin your most precious relationships. You can be freed from being controlled by your sin nature because God's son, Jesus Christ, frees you from sin through His death on the cross and resurrection from the dead. All you have to do is confess your sin, turn from it, and follow Christ's example for living like you've been chosen by God. All of who God is, His holiness, is available to you to keep your marriage the perfect, holy union it's designed to be. As your heavenly Father, God will give you the strength to resist the forces of nature and numerous temptations in this world that have crumbled far too many couples. Though you will both battle selfishness, you can choose the supernatural power of God's love to win over the temptation to be selfish. In Christ, your marriage can be built on a foundation that will stand the strongest of storms. Choosing God's love is the best choice for protecting your marriage against the forces of nature.

That's one topic you'll never get bored talking about.

FOR NEARLYWEDS

If destiny or fate brought you together, what then (according to this reasoning) is responsible for keeping you together? What are choices you both have made that have strengthened your relationship? What choices have led to hurt feelings? Talk about why selfishness is such a powerful force in relationships. What can you do to overcome selfishness in your marriage? How can the power of God help you overcome the power of selfishness?

FOR NEWLYWEDS

What choices did you make in deciding to marry one another? Once you're married, how does selfishness challenge those choices? Name one area in which you're tempted to be selfish. How can you overcome selfishness by building your marriage on the solid foundation of God's love?

Guys Want Lingerie, Not Lanz!

10

After sex, I mean the second after, she continues from where she left off. Her eyes open, and before you can breathe, you hear, ". . . and, oh yeah, I have to defrost the chicken, and your mother wants you to pick up her dry cleaning . . ."

—JIMMY, FORT LAUDERDALE, FLA.

Mrs. Newlywed, please allow me to be bold. I speak on behalf of your husband, all newly married men, and all not-so-newly married men like myself. Throughout the history of time, perhaps the greatest physical faculty we guys have developed is an acute sense of sight. In the optical arena, we are visual overachievers.

Our eagle-eye acuity explains why we have the capacity to sit for extended periods of time in front of a television set during every professional sports play-off, how we can spot every new scratch or door ding on the car the moment our wives pull into the driveway, and how we can sit one foot away from a computer screen surfing the Internet for hour after hour without going blind as we mumble every five minutes, "I'll be off in a minute; I'll be off in a minute." When we duck-hook our drives on the first hole, our 20-20 vision enables us to pinpoint the exact location of a golf ball lost in the high weeds. After three to four attempts, we have the ocular ability to see through walls and find the stud we are looking for to hang our wives' picture frames. And during the middle of the night, when the refrigerator is calling, our night vision enables us to stagger to the source of our stomach's longing without stumbling down the stairs or stepping on the cat.

Though we know you are riveted with the excellence of our eyesight and certainly pleased that we don't bring nyctalopia, strabismus, or ophthalmia into the marriage relationship, if there is one area in which we want to see eye to eye with you, without a doubt, it is the naked eye.

Starting today, on behalf of all newlywed guys, I am proclaiming a national campaign to celebrate Optical Awareness Month. This campaign is designed to remind our wives that we love it when you wear the skimpy lingerie we buy you. If you don't want to wear the lingerie we buy you, you can opt to celebrate Red Ribbon Week and wear only the red ribbon which we will gladly provide you. As visual overachievers, we are into packaging, and we love to unwrap our most treasured relationship.

Not only is Optical Awareness Month designed to promote lingerie longevity until the seventy-fifth wedding anniversary and the intense need we guys have to be held and hugged and snuggled and nurtured and cherished and loved, but it also has an equally important purpose of exposing the nefarious nemesis of newlywed nighties.

Lanz pajamas.

For the uninitiated, Lanz pajamas are the Martha Washingtons of wedding wear. They're the type of pajamas that Laura and Mary Ingalls went to bed in on the top bunk of *Little House on the Prairie.* Lanz pajamas are visual blindfolds for guys wanting to feast on the eye candy of alluring lingerie. One pair of Lanz pajamas is approximately the same size as an Olympic racing sloop spinnaker. Lanz are wedding gifts from mothers-in-law who fear for their daughters on the wedding night. We say, "Lose the Lanz."

Taking off lingerie is quick and easy. Just what a guy likes. Taking off a pair of Lanz is like pulling the sheets off the bed to do the wash. Not only do Lanz pajamas block your husband's point of view, these flannel jammies are flammable fire hazards. Set aflame, one pair of Lanz pajamas is equal to a three-alarm fire at an Alabama textile factory.

On behalf of all optically aware guys, please do not wear Lanz on your wedding night or any time your husband is not away on an overnight business trip. Women wear lingerie, and little girls wear Lanz. Unless your new husband has fallen through the ice as you hunt for sturgeon on your honeymoon, in which case wrapping his frozen, hypothermic body in Lanz may save his life, Lanz has no practical use.

As part of our Optical Awareness Month campaign, I've written an educational piece designed to inform the pajama-prone public on the benefits of lingerie and the liabilities of Lanz.

Pro-Lingerie	Anti-Lanz
Lingerie is visually appealing to men.	Lanz pajamas are visually appealing if you need curtains for large bay windows.
Lingerie accents a woman's figure.	Lanz pajamas make a woman look like she's wearing a Coleman sleeping bag to bed.
Lingerie makes guys hot-blooded.	Lanz keeps a woman cold-blooded.
Lingerie is quick and easy to take off.	Lanz is like trying to dismantle a pup tent in the wind.
Lingerie makes a bride look like a woman.	Lanz makes a bride look like Imohoptep, the mummified daughter of Ramses II.
Lingerie comes in all shapes and sizes.	Lanz, like potato sacks, comes only in XXL.
Lingerie creates a mood of excitement.	Lanz makes guys moody.
Lingerie is dangerously fun.	Lanz is plain old dangerous. Last year, thousands of guys died from Lanz suffocation.
Lingerie leads to great sex.	Lanz leads to lint-covered husbands.
Lingerie keeps a marriage alive and free.	Lanz keeps a marriage wrapped in material-ism.

Raising the bedroom banner of lingerie versus Lanz is one of the important marriage missions of this book, but in all respect to women who want a fair and balanced treatment of honeymoon scenarios, I am willing to address what some brides consider to be the gruesome grooming habits of guys. In my extensive research to help newlyweds honeymoon their way to wedded wonder, I originally thought all bridal magazines were written for women on topics pertaining exclusively to women. But, what I discovered is that many of the articles are stealth propaganda to help future husbands with the basic hygiene skills they don't teach in fraternities or the military.

Flipping through one bridal magazine to the next, I came across article after article written for women designed to get their guy ready for the Big Day. Tucked between the whip-your-wedding-guy-into-sanitary-shape articles were 1,573,984 pictures of beautiful single women wearing new bridal gowns for June 1 weddings. For all June 2 weddings, there were 1,872,179 bridal gown photos. On an annual basis, you can see just how big this wedding market really is. In fact, depending on sales of this book, I'm considering a secondary career in wedding gown fashion design, but I'm off on a bunny trail now, aren't I?

Guys, if we want our wives to wear lingerie, we have to give them a reason to want us. Based upon solid *Brides* magazine research, here's a list of actual grooming gross-outs our wives would like us to change before they even consider hopping into bed with us.[1] Where appropriate, I will provide my own commentary to these at times ridiculous female solutions to what amounts to blatant male makeovers.

Girl Gripe: Planet of the Apes. "He's got hair sprouting out his ears and nose. Yuck!"

***Brides'* Solution:** Try waxing or electrolysis.

Commentary: And why didn't you tell him this before you got engaged? No guy, no matter how much he loves you, is going to go for hot wax up his nose. Concerning electrocution, no matter how you try to change a guy, five million gigawatts won't work.

---

[1] Conde Nast, "13 Grooming Gross-Outs Solved," *Brides*, November/December 1999. The author would like to point out that this article failed to point out the male proclivity for nose, naval, toe, and zit picking.

Girl Gripe: Unibrow. "He thinks eyebrow maintenance is a girls-only thing, but his unibrow is not sexy."

***Brides'* Solution:** Tweezerman's Point Tweezer for precision plucking.

Commentary: I say go into the guy's garage and grab his belt sander.

Girl Gripe: Smell from Hell. "After exercise or major stress, he stinks. And he actually seems proud of the rank odors his body sends out."

***Brides'* Solution:** A good shower and antiperspirant.

Commentary: Guys may have cornered the market on all things foul and stinky, but a simpler solution is for women to stand upwind. It will save water during a drought.

TOGETHER FOREVER

You can spend a lot of time and energy getting groomed for a romantic evening alone, but if you really want to have a good sex life, it's important to understand that sexual intimacy is the icing on the cake of a solid, loving marriage. Before setting foot into the bedroom, there are things that every guy needs to know about women and things every woman needs to know about guys. Getting groomed for a lifelong sexual relationship with one another is a whole lot more than slipping on some slinky lingerie or plucking those disgusting nose hairs. To have your wedding cake and eat it too means you both must be willing to find out what lights your spouse's fire.

Guys, more than anything else, your new bride wants to know that she is numero uno on your list. Her highest need in her marriage to you is emotional intimacy. She wants to connect with you and to feel connected to you. If she calls you at your office to say hi and see how you're doing, the appropriate response is not, "What? Why are you calling me here?"

If your wife works in a corporate or professional office, she'll want to tell you about her day. If she's a professional stay-at-home mom, she'll want to tell you about her day. If she's an African bush pilot, she'll want to radio home and tell you about her day. If she's an engineer on a nuclear submarine, she'll want to ping you and tell you about her day. If she's a CIA operative in Whatchimacallistan, she'll want to call you on her satellite phone and tell you about her day. In the last case, of course, she may have to kill you, but you're getting the picture, aren't you?

Studies have documented the difference between how many words guys speak in a day and how many words women speak in a day. On an average day, a guy speaks about twelve words. Depending if the coffee maker is set the night before or not, he may reach as high as twenty-five words. A woman, on the other hand, speaks about 3.2 million words in a day, which may include an additional million or so if there's been a nasty fight among her girlfriends. So you can see the disparity between a guy's need to fulfill his DWC (Daily Word Count) and a woman's need to fulfill her DWC.

Guys, if you really work on helping your wife fulfill her DWC, you will stand head and shoulders above all the other newly married guys you know. If you sincerely listen to your wife, you will be praised above all men. Wives love to be listened to because it registers on their radar screens that you care about what's important to them. When you listen to your wife, you help create an atmosphere of security in your marriage. One of the greatest goals you can shoot for as a husband is to provide your wife with an overwhelming sense of security in your relationship. Granted, your wife is her own person, and you can't *make* her feel secure if she's carried a number of personal insecurities into your marriage, but there are plenty of things you can do to make your marriage a safe place for her to grow and to develop as a new wife. Don't throw yourself into your job, your sports, your hobbies, or your pet projects without involving your wife or allowing her to give her input. Listening to your wife and connecting with her day is the singularly greatest way to woo her.

Along with listening to your wife, ask yourself, *What does my wife really love? What makes her feel special and cared for? What does she appreciate more than anything else? If there were one thing I could do to make her day, what would it be? What is her favorite restaurant? Her favorite type of flowers? Her favorite perfume? Her favorite music?*

Oh yeah, along with emotional intimacy, your wife will love it if you help around the home with a good attitude. You can plan the most perfect, enchanting, romantic date at the most expensive and exquisite restaurant in town—all in preparation for the after-dinner dessert of vigorous lovemaking—but if you forget to bring in the trash cans like she reminded you four times, you might as well pick out a good novel to read tonight.

As my friends Scott and Phil say, wooing a woman is like trying to plan an outside concert without a good weather forecast.

One cloud in the sky. One drop of rain.

One wrong look. One wrong comment.

One wrong note. And the whole concert is canceled.

Ladies, though we guys may forget and stumble along the way trying to remember how important your need is to feel emotionally connected, our strongest need is *to be physically connected*. When we say we like you in lingerie, WE MEAN IT! We have an acute sense of sexual sight, and we like to use it as often as possible. Leave the tent-making to Omar and wrap yourself in something that accents the body God gave you. You are the single choice we made for a lifetime of love and physical intimacy, so if it sounds like we've got jet fuel for testosterone, WE DO! When we said, "To have and to hold," we were talking about sex, weren't we?

Despite what many women may think, a guy doesn't have a high need for sex just for sex's sake. Close maybe, but that's not the whole picture. When a guy has an active and healthy sex life with his wife, the physical act of sex is a major contributing factor to his sense of emotional health with his wife and his marriage. A guy is wired for sex just like a woman is wired for emotional intimacy. That's not to say that women don't have high sexual appetites or that men don't have strong emotional needs, because neither need is mutually exclusive. But, in a strict ranking of priorities, guys will definitely take sex over coffee and conversation.

Whether it's lingering over a latte together or livening your marriage with a little lingerie, the best way to have your wedding cake and eat it too is to make a regular practice of communicating your physical and emotional needs to one another. Sex, love, and romance are essential parts of married life, but they only happen when you communicate with one another. Asking each other who needs what and when are conversation starters that will keep your love for each other alive and growing.

I'm convinced that a healthy sex life can only be as good as the quality of the relationship between a husband and wife who support it. Sexual and emotional intimacy are gifts from God that we are privileged to share with each other, but like everything else in having your wedding cake and eating it too, it takes work to make these areas as good as they can be. With gentleness and healthy amounts of understanding, you can honor one another by seeking your spouse's best interests first. If you truly work on giving to one another emotionally and physically, you're bound to wrap your marriage in something much better than lingerie or Lanz.

FOR NEARLYWEDS

Believe it or not, many couples don't talk about sex before their wedding night. Have you? What are you looking forward to? What apprehensions do you have? What will prepare you to understand each other's physical and emotional needs before your wedding night?

FOR NEWLYWEDS

So how was it, and how is it? A lot of newlyweds experience sexual frustration and tension as they work on developing a sexual relationship. Husbands, are you in tune with your wife's emotional needs? What are they? Wives, are you in tune with your husband's sexual needs? In which areas do you both need to understand and to compromise with one another to have the best relationship possible?

Opposite Families Do Attract

11

Every family tree has to have some sap.

You don't have to be married for very long before you realize that everything you thought you knew about the person you married is completely wrong.

Okay, that may be a little extreme. Maybe you were only partially wrong.

When you were dating, you thought you knew your fiancée better than anyone else in the whole wide world and that your fiancée knew you better than anyone else in the whole wide world. You were so compatible. You finished each other's sentences. You laughed at each other's silly jokes. You were amazed to discover you both liked the same cartoons as kids. You called each other in the wee hours of the morning just to hear each other's voices. You stared into each other's eyes to see who would blink first. You loved the same restaurants, you watched the same movies, and you exchanged your favorite books. Then one day, you exchanged each other's rings.

I don't doubt for one second that when you were dating you were very compatible. I mean, after all, compatibility is one of the major reasons people get married. But, when you were dating and engaged, you were also on your best behavior. Who would ever think to say, "Hi! I'm a complete slob. Will you marry me?" or who would ever respond, "Yes, I'd love to marry you, but you first have to understand that I am the most anal-retentive person you've ever met in your life."

People who are that honest are single. For obvious reasons.

Even though you thought you knew the person you married better than anyone else, you would have saved yourself a lot of time to find out what your future spouse was really like by looking in his or her closet. Think about it: If you knew your future husband or wife was going to make the decision whether to marry you based upon looking in your closet, you would have whipped that fire hazard into shape quicker than you can say "I do."

Your closet looked like a Goodwill disposal bin. Clothes were arranged on the floor in order of dirty, semidirty, and suitable with no smell. The plastic wrappings from the dry cleaners covered the pile of wool sweaters in the corner, but that saved you from having to buy a cedar-lined sweater chest. It did, however, kill a whole family of mice that you repeatedly told not to play with the plastic. Your shoes, none of which could be matched, were covered in dust. Had the fire department ever needed to break into your apartment to rescue you from the avalanche of ancient guy artifacts that clobbered you from the top shelf, you would have been fined more than what it cost to pay for your wedding.

You were keeping that little secret of your life in the closet where it belonged, but you would have also learned a little about your fiancée by looking into her closet. Had you done so, you would have discovered an amazing sight that represented a psychological profile of the woman you were about to marry.

Shirts, pants, and dresses ironed. Arranged in correct color palate order. Exactly one inch apart.

Shoes neatly arranged by color, style, and heel height. Matching belts and purses directly above. Date of last time worn in public on clipboard.

Socks and underwear placed in perfect order, according to day of the week.

Okay, so maybe you never addressed the issue of closet compatibility before you got married, but hey, who does? All you cared about was that you knew that you and your true love were compatible, and you figured you could work out the closet kinks once you got married.

Maybe you were drawn to your future spouse because he or she was so different from you. After all, you reasoned, opposites do attract. Do opposites attract? You got me. All I know is that some people are intrigued by other people who are completely unlike them. That's usually where the trouble begins.

Say you two newlyweds are making dinner together. You ask him to wrap the dinner rolls in aluminum foil and stick them in the oven. As you slice the carrots to put in the salad, you glance over your shoulder to see if he's doing it the right way. Astounded by what you see, you quickly take control of the situation.

"No, no, no, honey . . . when you wrap the dinner rolls in aluminum foil, the shiny side always stays on the outside."

He looks at you like you just traveled ten thousand light years from the planet Endor. "No, no, no, dear . . . the dull side goes on the outside. Everybody knows the heat conducts better and the rolls stay warmer when the dull side is facing out."

You look at him like he's got a tapeworm coming out of his nose. "No, no, no, no, nobody you know, darling, knows anything about the right way to heat dinner rolls."

After a pleasant dinner of soup, salad, fried chicken, and unheated dinner rolls as the only way to solve your culinary incompatibility, you both pitch in to do the dishes together. How hard can it be to get the dishes done with two people?

"Why did you put the silverware in upside down?"

"I didn't put it in upside down. I put it in RIGHTSIDE DOWN!"

"The forks, knives, and spoons won't get clean that way!"

"The silverware is placed down so you don't stab yourself when you unload it."

"But they won't get clean!"

"Then run the dishwasher twice!"

"Do you know how wasteful that is? Don't you care about our planet?"

After leaving the dishes in the sink, you both decide to go to bed after your romantic evening of fighting over flatware and foil folding. But going to bed is not as simple as it sounds. Bedtime rituals are highly ingrained habits dating back to each of your respective childhoods. As you both stand at the sink, you soon discover that your distinctive way of doing things is not limited to forks and foil.

"Do you always floss before you brush?"

"Only after chewing a wad of aluminum foil. Yes, I always floss before I brush."

"You're supposed to brush, rinse, then floss."

"Who says?"

"My dad. He didn't go to dental school for nothing, you know."

"Didn't your dad ever tell you that flossing gets the big chunks out first? If you brush, rinse, then floss, you might still have big chunks in your mouth after you floss."

"Whatever."

"Don't 'whatever' me! First it's foil! Then forks! Now floss!"

A flippant *whatever* usually doesn't go over very well with a frustrated spouse trying to fix your flagrant flossing ways. If you've been feeling fatigued by the failure of your fickle spouse to change his or her favorite, fallacious way of doing things, you're not alone in fearing you're the only one who thinks or feels this way. The actual root of the frequent frustrations found in the first few years of marriage is not to be found in your spouse, but in the family your spouse came from. And I'm here to let you in on a dirty little secret.

Your spouse's family had a funny way of doing things.

It doesn't matter if you and your spouse were completely compatible when you were dating or if you were drawn together because opposites attract. The one sure thing you can count on when you get married is *opposite families do attract.* In almost every area imaginable in marriage, your spouse's family had a funny way of doing things. The very things that drive you crazy about your spouse are the same things that were normal and natural in the way he or she was raised. There are a lot of different ways to make sure the dishes get clean, but you can bet that your paper plates are going to furl some eyebrows for somebody raised on heated plates and the finest of flatware. Don't believe me? Whether it's foil, flatware, or floss, your families both had a funny way of doing things.

His Family Did It This Way	Her Family Did It That Way
His mom served pizza, Chinese, Mexican, hamburgers, and subs. Takeout, that is.	Her mom made fresh-cooked meals every night. Dinner at 6:00. Don't dare be late.
His dad restores demolished cars and builds boats barehanded and blindfolded.	Her dad couldn't fix his way out of a paper bag. That's what repairmen are for.
His parents get everything on sale.	Her parents pay retail for everything.
His family thinks vacation means camping in the dirt for a week.	Her family thinks it's only a vacation if you travel out of the country.
His parents think the only way to argue is to scream like howling monkeys.	Her parents never argued. *(Liars.)*
His family always celebrated New Year's and every major holiday.	Her family went to bed at 9:00 on New Year's and found no fun in festivity.
His dad screamed, "Who left the light on in this room?"	Her dad left every light on in the house to ward off prowlers.
His family had a TV in every room and memorized the TV guide like scripture.	Her family went to museums and art shows.
His family paid cash for everything.	Her family was on a first-name basis with every major credit-card company.
His mom always cleaned his room.	Her mom didn't let her go anywhere till her room was clean.
His family played board games for fun.	Her family competed to the death.
His family was always late.	Her family was as punctual as a Swiss watch.
His family loves a good prank.	Her family is nice and would never think of doing anything remotely unkind.
His family is as avant-garde as a Parisian fashion show.	Her family is as traditional as British royalty.
His family always buys each other gifts, and you are bathroom scum if you don't.	Her family never buys each other gifts.
His family invited everybody over to the house at all hours of night and day.	Her family had prearranged guest lists.
His family celebrates birthdays like a global event.	Her family thinks birthdays are no big deal.

TOGETHER FOREVER

You only find out how different you both really are after you get married and get under each other's skin by trying to retrain one another with the right way of doing things. Every newly married couple does it. I don't care if it's screwing in a light bulb, closing the lid on a cereal box, turning off the lights in every room, wiping off the table after every meal, dusting the furniture, slicing vegetables, or balancing a checkbook, every couple brings their strange and peculiar ways of doing things into the marriage. And it all comes from the funny family in which they were raised. If you're having trouble understanding your new husband or wife, you don't have to look any farther than his or her family. If you've ever wondered . . .

Why does she have to balance to the penny?

Why does he dump his clothes all over the place?

Where did she get this idea about cleaning everything twice?

How can a grown man act like such a big baby?

Why does she have to call her mom ten times in a day?

Why does he get so mad when I want to call a repairman?

The majority of all of your attitudes, habits, idiosyncrasies, customs, routines, and ingrained ideas about how to do things come from or are in response to not your new spouse but the family you grew up in. Though you are a unique individual with your own personality, temperament, belief systems, preferences, likes and dislikes, desires and needs, much of who you are was shaped by the parents who raised you. While some of the ways you do certain things are useful and productive, and others may be wasteful and unproductive, you can count on your spouse's way being different than your way.

What makes common sense to you makes complete nonsense to your spouse.

If you want to sort through and smooth out the spousal squabble of "whose way is the right way" that is common to all newlyweds, here are a few thoughts to keep in mind.

Understand That Opposite Families Do Attract. Your family and your spouse's family may not be complete opposites in every manner or behavior, but they certainly will be different. Like every marriage, every family is unique. The things that attracted you to your spouse will lead to new discoveries of things you find unattractive or even annoying about your spouse. Trying to understand the family your spouse came from just might help you understand how your new bride or groom is wired.

If your husband loves to spend hours working on his car in the garage, it may be because his dad spent hours in the garage working on his car. Though it might be easy to misinterpret his motor obsession as a message that he doesn't want to spend time with you, your husband is probably just doing something he grew up doing.

If your wife loves to invite people over and spends hours in the kitchen preparing for meals when you'd rather go to the gym together, it's probably because she came from a family that loved to cook and to have company over.

How your family handled conflict was different from how your spouse's family handled conflict. How your family handled money was different from how your spouse's family handled money. How your family communicated with one another was different from how your spouse's family communicated with one another. What was extremely important to your family may not be very important to your spouse's family. The big issues in your family may be nonissues in your spouse's family. Almost every area of family life is marked by the differences in how you and your spouse were raised, and the challenge of starting your new life together is understanding these family differences instead of being divided by them.

Be Open to Learning from Your Spouse. I have a confession to make. When I got married at age twenty-five, I had never once balanced my checking account. No, not even once! And guess where Krista worked when we were dating? You got it . . . *at a bank.* My philosophy of money management was save some, spend some, give some, and let the spare change fall where it may. As long as I knew I had money in my checking account and wasn't bouncing checks like Tiggers do best, I didn't worry about balancing.

To which Krista would reply, "But how do you know how much money you have if you don't balance your checkbook? Or what if the bank makes an error?"

I can see the strength in your logic, O Wise One.

So when Krista and I got married and opened a joint checking account, I was convinced by her line of reasoning, along with marrying two incomes, that it made a lot of sense to balance our dollars and cents. Since I've been married and have changed my loose-change money-management ways, I now go crazy when I don't balance to the penny. I do all of our financial management and on-line banking on Quicken. I love reading about investing and learning new ways to be a better manager of our resources. Now this change didn't happen because I'm a financial wise guy. It came because I wasn't threatened to learn something new from Krista and the values she was raised with. Like any other couple, Krista and I don't always see dime to dime on how to spend a buck. Just this very second, she walked into my office and proudly told me how she scored big time on a 75-percent-off sale at her favorite gift store. *Oh no,* I groaned. *Here it comes . . .*

"And I bought two hundred dollars' worth of gifts!"

Okay, so she spent more than I would, but in the long run, she saved us a bundle on gifts over the next year. But don't you dare tell any of her friends that the twenty-dollar candle (next year's Christmas gift) only cost us five bucks.

Be open to learning from each other. Each of you brings strengths, talents, abilities, and giftedness to your marriage. Recognize that the family your spouse was raised in has different values, beliefs, and ways of doing things, but some of these things are worth learning and incorporating into your own life.

Recognize There Are a Lot of Ways to Do the Same Things. How the dinner rolls are warmed, which direction to place the flatware, or how you handle your dental hygiene is usually a matter of preference not right or and wrong. For instance, take dinner rolls. It makes absolutely no difference whether you wrap dinner rolls in aluminum foil with the shiny side on the outside or inside. Heat is not conducted better one way or the other. What most people don't know, and one of the most amazing discoveries you'll make in this book, is that when aluminum foil is manufactured, the foil comes off the metal rollers in large sheets. One side is shiny and the other side is dull because of how it rolls off the roller. Inside or out, heat is conducted the same way. (That little tidbit alone is worth the price of this book!)

But, how much heat is cooked up in the kitchen or in any other room of the house when my way is the right way and your way is the wrong way? Most of the time, there are a lot of ways to do the same thing, but since we'd prefer to be right about our preference to stir soup with a bona fide soup ladle instead of a spatula, it's easier to try to show our spouse the error of his or her ways. Instead of insisting on your way to get things done, allow your spouse the space to accomplish tasks in a way that works for them. Don't put your husband or wife into a Spousal Retraining Program. The dropout rate is very high, and it does nothing to build a together-forever love for one another.

Be Willing to Change for Your Spouse. If there's honestly a better way to butter toast or balance the checkbook so you aren't getting hit with stiff bank fees, it's important to be willing to change for your spouse and for your marriage.

Some people enter marriage with the erroneous belief that "If my spouse truly loves me, I don't have to change. He/she should just accept me for who I am." Okay, then you and I can respond to the selfish, inconsiderate, immature, self-seeking sap that thinks this way, "Do you prefer Chinese water torture, the rack, or being locked in a small closet with seventies elevator music?"

Yes, we should accept and love our spouses for the unique

people that they are, but we should be willing to change and learn and grow for one another so our marriages can be the very best they can be. You can't have your wedding cake and eat it too if you're not willing to compromise and to change. Every person and every marriage, in one way or another, resists change, but if a marriage always stays the same, it will eventually die. Marriages are meant to change because marriage is a living, dynamic relationship. The only way a marriage moves forward is by the positive momentum that builds when a husband and wife work together by changing, adapting, and doing what it takes to keep the marriage healthy and alive. All change involves conflict, but you have to ask yourself whether it's the good type of conflict that creates positive changes or the negative type of conflict that keeps you both dug into your defensive positions until the marriage itself begins to circle the drain.

When you're willing to change for your spouse, you send a loud-and-clear message that you care about what your spouse thinks and feels. Your willingness to learn, flex, and find new ways to do things shows you place a higher value on marriage unity than refusing to get off your own little unicycle. Sure, you may raise an eyebrow or wonder why your spouse makes such a big deal about parking where the car won't get door dings, but in the grand scheme of things, does it really matter? By not making a big deal about changing how or why you do something the way you do, you'll be well on your way to becoming a very attractive spouse.

FOR NEARLYWEDS

What are your fiancée's unique likes, dislikes, and preferences for doing things a certain way? How are these preferences related to how he or she was raised? How do you tend to think and act like your parents? Why is it so important to identify your similarities and your differences before you get married?

FOR NEWLYWEDS

What do you find unbelievable about the way your husband or wife does something? How is this related to his or her upbringing? What positive traits or ways of doing something have you learned from your spouse so far? How can being open to changing for your spouse help develop a together-forever love?

There's Somebody in My Bed

12

A man meets a genie. The genie tells him he can have whatever he wants, provided that his mother-in-law gets double. The man thinks for a moment and then says, "Okay, give me a million dollars and beat me half to death."

Since you got married and began sleeping in the same bed with your beloved, have you ever woken up out of a deep sleep in the middle of the night and grabbed the sheets with the frightening thought, *Oh my gosh! There's somebody in my bed!*

Did you leave the door unlocked? Did someone slip through an open window? Was a sick, demented soul hiding in the closet before you got home? As you slowly and quietly reach underneath the bed for your Louisville Slugger baseball bat, you pray for the strength to impale the intruder in your bed with all the power of a six-year-old taking on a birthday piñata. You slowly wrap your fingers around the grip. You gently stand up in the bed, careful not to wake the sleeping psychopath. You raise the bat high above your head, and as you begin your ferocious downswing, it suddenly dawns on you that the person you're about to pummel is wearing a wedding ring.

Ka-wham!

You barely miss. Pillow feathers cloud the room.

"Ugh! What are you doing? Put down that bat! You're going to hurt someone!"

"Sorry, dear. I thought you were somebody else."

You're married, but you're still thinking single.

Or what about when you first started changing your clothes in front of your new husband or wife? Depending on the person, it takes anywhere from six seconds to sixty years for husbands and wives to become completely comfortable changing in front of one another. In the dressing-room area of marriage, there are generally two types of spouses.

The first is the Brazen Spouse. The Brazen Spouse is the newly married spouse who drops his or her clothes for shock value. Brazen Spouses are the same people who, as little kids, were always taking off their clothes when company came over. So you can imagine the sheer delight of a Brazen Spouse when his or her new spouse shrieks at the sight of a naked body doing jumping jacks in the living room moments before the in-laws walk through the door for dinner.

The Brazen Spouse has his or her roots in one of two generations. The first generation the Brazen Spouse identifies with is the sixties generation, when everyone was taking off their clothes, except President Johnson. The Brazen Spouse reasons that all body parts basically look the same, clothes are a nuisance, dry cleaning is expensive, and nobody likes to iron, so why wear clothes at all? The second generation the Brazen Spouse readily identifies with is the seventies generation, when people leftover from the sixties made the amazing discovery that not only did not wearing clothes give them that light, airy feeling of freedom, but that they could also run much faster without clothes. Hence, the birth of streaking.

The polar opposite of the Brazen Spouse in the newlywed dressing room is the Bashful Spouse. The Bashful Spouse, I'm pretty sure about this, has *never even seen* his or her own body. The Bashful Spouse not only goes into a locked bathroom to get away from the Brazen Spouse, who's now holding a spatula for a microphone and doing Frank Sinatra "Love and Marriage" karaoke on the kitchen table, but the Bashful Spouse flips the light off and changes in the dark. The Bashful Spouse is an expert at changing under a wet bath towel, behind the shower curtain, and underneath the bed covers. And if the Brazen Spouse has gone too loopy, the Bashful Spouse will resort to changing underneath the bed. If you married a Bashful Spouse, you can forget about making love with the lights on. A full moon, however, can be a suitable compromise.

Now what drives a Bashful Spouse absolutely crazy is when the Brazen Spouse tries to catch the Bashful Spouse in the act of changing (in this case) her clothes. The Brazen Spouse loves to sneak up on an unsuspecting Bashful Spouse when her full moon is shining and give it a really good pinch! *Yeeooww!* The Bashful Spouse will grab her burning bum, while at the same time trying to perform a defensive "duck-and-cover" maneuver to ward off any secondary attacks like tickling, wet willies, or Indian burns. The Bashful Spouse's defensive maneuvers aren't really necessary because by now, the Brazen Spouse is rolling on the ground naked in hysterical laughter, fully pleased with his successful surprise attack that he thought was just so funny. What's really funny, though, is the look on the Brazen Spouse's face when he looks up and sees his new in-laws staring at him through the front window. Early again.

Getting used to having a stranger in your bed or trying to slap off a brazen, bum-pinching spouse are only a couple of the changes that come with getting married. Not only does marriage force you to change your lifestyle in so many ways, you sometimes even have to change your way of thinking, particularly if you're hanging on to any dated ideas of the way marriage used to be. I don't know which generation you identify with the most, but I hope it's something a little more recent than the fifties generation. Check out the e-mail I received some time ago: The following excerpt is from an actual home-economics textbook from the fifties, intended to teach high-school girls how to prepare for married life:

1. *Have dinner ready.* Plan ahead, even the night before, to have a delicious meal on time. This is a way of letting

him know that you have been thinking about him and are concerned about his needs. Most men are hungry when they come home, and the prospects of a good meal are part of the warm welcome needed.

2. *Prepare yourself.* Take fifteen minutes to rest so you will be refreshed when he arrives. Touch up your makeup, put a ribbon in your hair, and be fresh looking. He has just been with a lot of work-weary people. Be a little gay and a little more interesting. His boring day may need a lift.

3. *Clear away clutter.* Make one last trip through the main part of the house just before your husband arrives, gathering up schoolbooks, toys, paper, etc. Then run a dustcloth over the tables. Your husband will feel he has reached a haven of rest and order, and it will give you a lift too.

4. *Prepare the children.* Take a few minutes to wash the children's hands and faces. If they are small, comb their hair, and if necessary, change their clothes. They are little treasures, and he would like to see them playing the part.

5. *Minimize the noise.* At the time of his arrival, eliminate all noise of washer, dryer, or vacuum. Try to encourage the children to be quiet. Greet him with a warm smile and be glad to see him.

6. *Some DON'TS.* Don't greet him with problems or complaints. Don't complain if he's late for dinner. Count this as minor compared with what he might have gone through that day.

7. *Make him comfortable.* Have him lean back in a comfortable chair or suggest he lie down in the bedroom.

Have a cool or warm drink ready for him. Arrange his pillow and offer to take off his shoes. Speak in a low, soft, soothing, and pleasant voice. Allow him to relax and unwind.

8. *Listen to him.* You may have a dozen things to tell him, but the moment of his arrival is not the time. Let him talk first.

9. *Make the evening his.* Never complain if he does not take you out to dinner or to other places of entertainment; instead, try to understand his world of strain and pressure and his need to be home and relax.

10. *The Goal:* Try to make your home a place of peace and order where your husband can relax.

Now before you say anything, I already know what you guys are thinking, and from many years of having my cake and eating it too, I know exactly what you women are also thinking. You guys are thinking, *So what's the big deal? Sounds good to me. The fifties was a wonderful generation. Hot muscle cars. Elvis. Leather jackets.* Guys, the women are already one up on us. Here is the second half of the e-mail, and they have put up a formidable defense.

THE UPDATED VERSION FOR THE TWENTY-FIRST-CENTURY WOMAN

1. *Have dinner ready.* Make reservations ahead of time. If your day becomes too hectic, just leave him a voice mail message regarding where you'd like to eat and at what time. This lets him know that your day has been crummy and gives him an opportunity to change your mood.

2. *Prepare yourself.* A quick stop at the Clinique counter on your way home will do wonders for your outlook and will keep you from becoming irritated every time he opens his mouth. (Don't forget to use his credit card!)

3. *Clear away the clutter.* Call the housekeeper and tell her that any miscellaneous items left on the floor by the children can be placed in the Goodwill box in the garage.

4. *Prepare the children.* Send the children to their rooms to watch television or play Nintendo. After all, both of them are from his previous marriage.

5. *Minimize the noise.* If you happen to be home when he arrives, be in the bathroom with the door locked.

6. *Some DON'TS.* Don't greet him with problems and complaints. Let him speak first, and then your complaints will get more attention and remain fresh in his mind throughout dinner. Don't complain if he's late for dinner; simply remind him that the leftovers are in the fridge, and you left the dishes for him to do.

7. *Make him comfortable.* Tell him where he can find a blanket if he's cold. This will really show you care.

8. *Listen to him.* But don't ever let him get the last word.

9. *Make the evening his.* Never complain if he does not take you out to dinner or other places of entertainment; instead, go with a friend or go shopping (use his credit card). Familiarize him with the phrase "Girls' Night Out!"

10. *The Goal:* Try to keep things amicable without reminding him that he thinks the world revolves around him. Obviously he's wrong; it revolves around you.

TOGETHER FOREVER

I've talked with a lot of newlyweds, and if there's one common thread that's consistent in most of my conversations, it's this: *Many couples underestimate just how drastic the transition is from singlehood to marriagedom.* For some couples, getting married is a smooth and enjoyable transition. These couples glide right into marriage as if they just walked off the top of a wedding cake. For other couples, getting married is like getting so much cake smeared in your face you can't see straight. It's a difficult transition marked with a lot of confusion and conflict, not because you don't love each other, but because there's been so much change all at once. Where do you fit?

You know in your head that marriage is a major life change, but in your heart, you may sometimes wonder if you can handle so much change at once. Yes, there are all sorts of changes and transitions in living together—deciding who's going to pay the bills, who's going to do which chores, and all the other stuff I make fun of in this book—but a major change like marriage can bring other major changes as well. Here are just some of the double-whammy changes you might be adjusting to as a newlywed . . .

Did you get married and move out of your folks' home for the first time? Or might you have married and moved across the country? Perhaps you married right out of college or high school, which are big enough transitions even without a wedding cake. Or maybe you just got married and started a new job right when you returned from your honeymoon? Or are you married and still trying to finish school? Maybe you're married and all of your good friends are still single? Or were you single for a long time with a professional career and now your marriage is the biggest change in a long time?

To navigate the changes of being newly married and to truly know that "for better or worse" is not a curse, it's important to understand how powerful the force of change is in your life. Having your wedding cake and eating it too means you have to take a realistic look at the changes of married life and how those changes are impacting your relationship.

Take a "Change Assessment." Look at your life right now and ask yourself, "How many things have changed in my life in the past three months? The past six months? The past year? Two years?" Life is filled with changes, and sometimes we underestimate how powerfully and dramatically those changes affect us. I've said before that nobody likes change except a wet baby. Marriage is an awesome enough life change without throwing in a move, a new job, the loss of a job, a death or serious illness in the family, or any other type of major conflict or disappointment. How much change has happened in your life? Taking a change assessment will help you orient yourself to where you are today. Identifying changes in your life can help you identify your feelings about those changes.

Change Produces Conflicting Feelings. Some changes are good and some are not-so-good, but no change is neutral. All change produces conflicting feelings. Getting married is a great and wonderful experience. You are gaining a friend, a soul mate, a confidant, a companion, and a lover for a lifetime. Marriage is a great change, and I'm all for it. But you know what? Marriage is a major life change, and believe it or not, marriage produces conflicting feelings. Marriage is the gain of a mate, but it's also saying sayonara to the single life. Now, you may have gladly said good-bye and good riddance to the single life, but the change I'm talking about is the loss of who you were as a single, unmarried person. Intrinsically, you're the same person with the same personality and temperament, but relationally, you are now a Mr. or a Mrs., and that is a major change! With your "Mr. and Mrs." title comes a whole new set of responsibilities, expectations, and roles that you never had before. You may be thrilled that you're married now, and I hope you are, but you may also be experiencing sadness, doubt, insecurity, jealousy, uncertainty, or anxiety like never before. And all these conflicting feelings, produced by the major change of getting married, can lead to conflict with the one to whom you said, "I do, I do, I do, I do, I do!" You won't be the first to think, *What was I doing when I said, "I do"?*

Watch Out for the Change Drain. When you change the oil in your car, you drain the old and put in the good. I wish there were a good Jiffy Lube for marriage. Being married, we know, is much more complicated than that. Constant, unmonitored change can drain a marriage quicker than a twenty-minute lube job. Guaranteed. As you assess the changes your marriage is going through, one thing you and your spouse will want to keep an eye on is how those changes are possibly draining your love for one another and your enthusiasm for your marriage. Too much change can be a major marriage drain.

I'm convinced that change is good for a marriage, because marriage is not a fixed, static relationship. A healthy marriage has to keep growing and changing to stay alive. Handled together as a team, change keeps a husband and wife growing, communicating, listening, understanding, compromising, setting goals, and exploring options that will ultimately keep the marriage alive and together forever. But too much change can also have the negative affect of one or both spouses choosing to pull away from each other. Instead of building a bridge to manage and to move through the change, what goes up instead is a major wall, and the couple reaches an impasse in their relationship.

Make Major Decisions Together. One of the best ways to navigate the many marriage changes that come your way is to commit to make all major decisions together. If you and your spouse want to keep your marriage from getting the life sucked out of it from too much change, be sure to seek each other's input for every major decision you face. Two heads are definitely better than one, so if you want to show your spouse how much you value him or her, involve your spouse in making decisions of significance. When couples work together as a team, especially when there are a lot of changes going on, each person is empowered to make his or her own contribution.

Pray and Seek Wise Counsel. Statistically speaking, couples who pray together stay together far longer than couples who don't. During seasons of change, prayer is the best way to calm an anxious heart. When you and your spouse pray together, you are able to take your eyes off your obstacles and put them on the Almighty Father, who never sleeps nor slumbers, who is the Author of all change yet who never changes. Ask Him for the wisdom and strength to deal with the changes in your marriage and the changes in the rest of your life that are affecting your marriage. The same God who will dress your marriage with the character qualities of strength, perseverance, and courage is the One who will guide you as you daily commit your lives to each other and to His will.

Don't forget about seeking the wise counsel of others whom you know and trust, who know you, and who are standing in your corner for your marriage. Take time to talk about the marriage changes on your mind with someone who has a marriage that you respect and admire. Good marriage counsel will go a long way to help you handle the changes that are a part of every marriage. And remember, through the coming years, your marriage will go through all sorts of changes. Some changes you'll be able to plan and prepare for; others will catch you naked as a jaybird. If you want to have your wedding cake and eat it too, as much as possible, try to anticipate, plan, and make the necessary changes needed to keep your marriage together forever. Be flexible with change and one another. After all, that person sleeping next to you is your spouse.

FOR NEARLYWEDS

What changes are you looking forward to in getting married? What changes are you unsure of or have questions about? When your marriage faces difficult changes, in what ways can you support one another?

FOR NEWLYWEDS

When you got married, which changes were pleasant surprises? Which changes caught you off guard or made you wish you were a little more prepared? What major or minor changes has your marriage gone through in the past year? When you're going through a personal change, what kind of support do you need from your husband or wife?

Marriage-Bed Rules

13

She snacks in bed. I sleep on the crumbs.
—Cary, Seattle, Wash.

You spend approximately one-third of your life in bed. Twenty-four hours in a day. An average of eight hours of sleep in a night. The numbers make sense.

All that changes when you get married.

In your first year of marriage, you'll spend a lot of time wrestling on top of or underneath the covers. A good wrestling match is one of marriage's most blessed entanglements. At least that's what you'll awkwardly tell your children when they walk in on you one day. Fabricate your story now. It's not a matter of "if." It's only a matter of "when":

Child: Mommy! What are you doing on top of daddy like that?

Mommy: Uh . . . uh . . . we're playing WWF Wrestlemania.

Child: But where are your jammies? YOU'RE BOTH NAKED! Hee, hee!

Mommy: This *is* my costume. I'm Electra, and I wear invisible body armor.

Daddy: That's right, and I'm Hairy Monster from *Sesame Street.*

Child: Hairy Monster has blue hair. Hairy Monster does not have black hair and white pimply skin like you, Daddy.

Mommy: Why don't we pop a video in for you, honey? Mommy and Daddy aren't finished wrestling.

Child: No way, I wanna play too. I'm Oscar the Grouch, the Trash Compactor.

Trying to cover up and cover your tracks puts a whole new spin on the words *bedtime story.* Store that video in your mind for future replay. Before getting too far ahead of myself by warning you about offspring intrusions during lovemaking, I do need to state the basics for marriage-bed rules.

Many premarital counselors are doing engaged couples a grave disservice by not adequately explaining the necessity of clearly posted rules for the marriage bed. Why these educated people with lots of misspelled words behind their names don't talk about marriage-bed rules absolutely baffles me. Freeways have posted signs and specific rules to abide by. Table saws have black-and-yellow warning stickers and posted rules. Chutes and Ladders, Monopoly, Scrabble, and Pretty, Pretty Princess all have rules to follow if somebody's going to win fair and square. There are playground rules. Rules at work. Rules at school. City, state, and federal rules. All nations are governed by rules, laws, and bylaws to prevent the reign of anarchy, looting in the streets, the disintegration of society, and cat doors being installed without Homeowner Association Board Approval. But I have yet to read anywhere about marriage-bed rules.

The marriage bed is where you will spend one-third of the rest of your life together with your new spouse. Shouldn't there be some sort of ground rules? A common understanding to prevent "newlybed" misunderstandings? If your premarital counselor didn't say anything about marriage-bed rules, I say you deserve a refund. You get a money-back guarantee if the marriage-bed rules aren't covered. If your counseling was free, well, you get what you pay for.

Some premarital counselors just don't like to get naked with revealing subjects like marriage-bed rules. They don't want to bare all out of fear of scaring some couples back into singlehood. But talking about marriage-bed rules isn't all that difficult. Ripping the covers off this sensitive subject should be as warm and inviting as easing into a warm spa.

Just the other day, I was sitting in a Jacuzzi by myself and came across a sign posted on a wall that explained the Jacuzzi rules. The sign read . . .

JACUZZI RULES

Shower before Entering
No Food or Drinks
Use Bathroom Facilities
No Children

As I lounged in the hot bubbly jets, I thought, *Hot tub! Jacuzzi rules are perfect marriage-bed rules!*

As soon as I read those Jacuzzi rules, I knew I was onto something big. Really big. Just think how you and your spouse can start your marriage off right by applying these simple rules every time you hop into bed. I'd sat in that Jacuzzi dozens of times before and never even considered that a perfect set of marriage-bed rules was right in front of my face. Oh, how the obvious eludes us! Now that I know the rules, I can help every marriage avoid the heartache, confusion, hurt feelings, and disgusting behaviors that are a direct result of mattress misunderstandings. If I had only had a simple, concise set of marriage-bed rules like the ones I'm going to give you now to post on the headboard above our heads, my marriage could've avoided a ton of trouble.

Shower before Entering. Hygiene matters. In one of my previous books, *Women Are Always Right and Men Are Never Wrong*, I dedicated a whole chapter to the subject of body odor. I firmly believe that a frank discussion about body odor should happen long before a couple gets engaged and that the subject of body odor should be a mandatory session in premarital counseling. Nothing will drive newlyweds to single beds or sleeping bags on the floor quicker than a bad case of body odor.

After a day's accumulation of sweaty perspiration coupled with the environmental pollutants of smog, dust, urban grime, pollen, Ortho weed killer, hairspray, fleas, ticks, Brut cologne, and biplane crop duster flybys, you'd think that your new husband or wife would have the common decency to shower before entering bed. But don't count on it. This is why we need marriage-bed rules. Get a whiff of this . . .

If you're a woman, before you get married, when your handsome fiancé arrives at your home all hot and sweaty from a five-mile run, he is sexy. Gorgeous. A real hunk. Once you get married and your new groom zooms in from jogging, you wonder why there's been no mention on the national news about evacuation procedures for a major biological accident.

If you're a guy, before you get married, when your fiancée works out, she doesn't perspire; she glistens. The sweat on her face sparkles like diamonds. Once you're married, your new bride returns from aerobics sweating like a sumo wrestler in a Japanese bathhouse. (The focus of the comparison here is sweat, not size.) Hey, newlyweds, here's some inspiration for marriage-bed perspiration: *Shower before Entering.* If it's that bad, hose off in the backyard and apply a liberal dusting of lime.

No Food or Drinks. When changing the sheets on your bed, there's nothing worse than snapping the sheets off and having nacho cheese Dorito crumbs, Oreo cookie innards, and rainbow-colored Skittles riddle your face like World War II antiaircraft fire. You may think I'm kidding, but I'm not. Pez candy makes for a dangerous projectile. Almost blinded me once. If you think that's bad, you should have seen the time I almost passed out from getting sour-gummy-worm dust up my nostrils. Absolutely scalding.

No food or drinks in the marriage bed. Period. Not only is it unhealthy to eat or drink before going to bed, it's downright dangerous for your sex life. What could be more humiliating for a guy whose new bride is forced to choose between him and chocolate? That's mental cruelty. If you and your new bride pop open a bottle of champagne on your wedding bed, who's going to be the designated driver? Ever feel how sharp the tip of a Dorito is? Get one of those under your back, and you'll see why you never want a spinal tap. For a healthy sex life, keep the marriage bed lean and no-cal.

Use Bathroom Facilities. Ladies, brace yourself. Your Prince Charming does have a chink in his armor, and it is strategically located in the lower posterior of his Underoos. Thanks to marrying a bona-fide shareholder of the world's largest natural gas company, you will no longer be needing your hair curlers or curling irons. Go ahead and throw them all away. You now have a husband who thinks he's Sir Poofus Maximus, and when you least expect it, he'll scream "Dutch Oven!" Before you have a second to react by donning a gas mask and biological warfare suit, you'll hear a low rumbling underneath your covers like the sound of distant thunder. As Armageddon approaches like the white-hot flash of nuclear winter, your metabolically challenged methane man will fluff the covers to blow you away with his incredible sense of humor. Ha-ha. Very funny. A real comedian.

Welcome to marriage.

That is, unless you beat him to it.

Gassy spouses are equal-opportunity destroyers.

If you want to light each other's fire, be careful what you wish for.

The simplest solution to make sure your spouse abides by the *Use Bathroom Facilities* rule is to keep a book of Ohio Blue Tip matches on your nightstand. Especially if you just went out for Mexican. You can use a lighter if you so desire, but I don't recommend storing two combustible materials (a lighter and a gassy spouse) so close together. It's the same principle as storing gasoline, oily rags, and paint thinner together in the garage. *Muy peligro.* Just to be on the safe side, it'd also be wise to tack a No Smoking sign on the bedpost. Once you sense or detect the slightest smell of your spouse trying to sneak one by, immediately grab a match.

Light it.

Make yourself perfectly clear. *"Stop or nobody gets outta here alive."*

You can do that, or think fire prevention first: Buy a bottle of Beano.

No Children. This marriage-bed rule should be self-explanatory, but it's not. Once you have kids, you might as well throw your marriage-bed rules out with the bathwater. It makes sense that children should not be allowed in Jacuzzis, especially if they can't swim. But biologically speaking, your children are born swimmers. As sperm, your children swan-dived into a small, circular egg. For the entire gestation period, they relaxed in their warm and watery World Wide Womb. The second the water broke, it was only a matter of time before they swam upstream and wound up in your bed. First comes breast-feeding at all hours of the night. (Guys, I'm serving notice here. You're familiar with the phrase "feast or famine"? Get ready for a new kind of diet.) After breast-feeding comes the terrible twos, which should really be characterized as "Three's a crowd."

Then you have nightmares. Monsters in the closet. Monsters under the bed. *The tree outside my window looks like a Reformed Party politician. I don't like that shadow. I hear a sound. I'm not tired. I need another drink. My nightlight just shorted out. I have to go potty. I went potty in my bed. I just threw up. My doll just threw up.* On and on it goes. Your kids will do anything to wiggle in bed with you. And then pee in it. If you're all nervous about having kids now, *relax.*

Letting your kids snuggle in bed is one of those rules worth breaking.

Minus the weewee.

Children are blessed proof that the marriage bed rules.

TOGETHER FOREVER

Before a Skittle snaps you in the eye or you start searching for gas masks in army surplus stores, let's make one thing perfectly clear: *The marriage bed rules.*

The marriage bed and everything that happens in it is one of the best things about married life. Long, intimate talks. Passionate love-making. Snuggling. Reading together. Watching your favorite TV show. Laughing. Talking about friends and family matters. Praying together. Falling asleep in each other's arms. The marriage bed is where you will spend a major part of your married life. Though most of your time will be spent sleeping, what you do with the rest of your "bedtime" makes an important difference in your relationship as husband and wife.

The marriage bed is a place where you'll spend a lot of time together, so it does make sense to talk with each other about how time spent on a mattress affects your marriage. Here's a list of conversation starters that you might find helpful as you both come up with your own creative set of marriage-bed rules.

Our Marriage Bed Is a Place Where We Freely Talk about Sex. Like any other aspect of your marriage, a healthy sexual relationship takes work and is definitely worth the work. Some couples get verbally frigid talking about sex, but communicating your thoughts and feelings about making love, what you like and don't like, what's pleasurable and not pleasurable, is just as important as any other part of your relationship.

Because sex is so personal, it can be an intimidating topic of conversation. Sex is incredibly enjoyable and mysterious. But because it's mysterious, we never completely figure it out. The mysterious nature of sex can be an incredible source of conflict for newly married and older married couples alike. That's why it's so important to consistently communicate with one another about sex. By honoring, listening, and respecting one another when you talk about sex, you can create a safe atmosphere to freely say what you need to say.

Our Marriage Bed Is a Place Where We Settle Conflicts Before Going to Sleep. Going to bed bitter, angry, and upset is a bad recipe for a good night's sleep. When your husband or wife is being a toad, turning your back and flopping your head on your pillow in a huff will only suffocate your chance of resolving the conflict before going to sleep. Make your marriage bed a place to resolve conflict before you go to sleep. Turn the light out on the problem, not on each other.

Not letting the sun go down on your anger gives your marriage a fresh start when you wake up in the morning. Go to sleep when you're ticked off at each other, and you will wake up to drink a bitter cup of day-old conflict. Unresolved conflict ruins relationships just like sour milk ruins a good cup of coffee. Stay up late if you have to.

Resolving your differences and forgiving one another before going to bed will give you both a chance to brew something hot and fresh in the morning.

Our Marriage Bed Is a Place Where We Talk about Our Lives. Krista and I love to read, so we always have our faces in a new book when we read in bed. But to get on the same page with one another, sometimes we have to put down our books and just talk. We need to connect. Talk about our day. Our high points. Our low points. Our joys. Our frustrations. Our dreams. It's easy to want to get lost in a novel and forget about the stress of the day, but it's also easy to get lost in marriage, so that's why our marriage bed is an intimate place where we spend a lot of time talking about what's important to us and to each other.

Make your marriage bed a place of intimacy by putting down your book or flipping off the TV. Reading or watching Leno may get you a few laughs, but it won't lead you to wedded wonder. When you lie down at night, you want to be on the same plane as your spouse because the marriage bed is the great leveler. It's the place to bare all and be all with the one person you've given your life to and who's given their life to you. It's the one place you'll never have to cover up, if you know the marriage-bed rules.

FOR NEARLYWEDS

A lot of couples go into their wedding night without having talked about sex. If you haven't yet talked about your sexual relationship and what your expectations, hopes, and desires are for your wedding night (and your marriage), now may be a good time to uncover this sexy topic.

FOR NEWLYWEDS

So far in married life, how would you describe your marriage-bed time together? What kinds of creative marriage-bed rules would maximize your mattress time together?

What to Do with Middle-of-the-Bed Fred

14

You cannot take your half of the bed from the middle.

In your first year of marriage, don't be surprised if you face all kinds of vexing and perplexing interpersonal challenges.

Wait a minute. Scratch that.

In your *first hour* of married life, you'll want to be wide-eyed with awareness for the confusing and confounding challenges nobody except me is going to prepare you for. From the get-go of getting off the altar, the first and most daunting challenge at your reception is pretending you know everyone you meet. This is where I think most political careers get started. If you're good enough and smooth enough, you just may be able to convince almost everyone at your wedding that you remember them as if you just spent the past twelve years of your life alone with each of them on a deserted island.

"Of course I remember you, Mrs. Ipsandorf! You're my mother's cousin's third-grade teacher's baby-sitter's boyfriend's sister's best friend from Kahoolawe, Hawaii, right?"

"No, I'm the bride's father's third wife's mother's bridge partner's hairdresser."

"Of course, how could I forget?"

There are, of course, many other marital challenges I could discuss in this chapter, but I think the best use of our time is talking about the newlywed challenge of bedtime. This topic is of such utmost importance to me that I am typing in my pink bunny jammies with the little vinyl-bottom footsies in order to frame my thoughts on the horizontal habits and hazards that can inflict undue stress on an otherwise harmonious marital relationship. Let's examine a few of the king-sized problems that far too many newlyweds are not properly equipped to deal with.

Which Side of the Bed Do You Want? Newlyweds, especially those on their wedding night, are nice and do not want to offend their spouses. New husbands, especially those who do not want to lose any sex privileges, will typically ask in a casual, nonchalant voice, "Which side of the bed do you want?" New brides, not wanting to offend their husbands, will respond, "Oh, it doesn't matter to me."

Let's pull the bedcovers off this one right away.

You do care.

You both care.

You either want the right side of the bed, the left side of the bed, or straight down the middle of the bed. Both of you came into marriage with very preconceived ideas of which side of the bed you wanted. Maybe it came from which side of the bed your mom or dad always slept on and the idea has been ingrained in your head: "Boys on the left and girls on the right." Maybe you're right-handed and superstitious. Anything remotely related to the left—staring into a cracked mirror, Jesse Ventura, walking under a ladder, stepping on a black cat, or sleeping on the left side of the bed—guarantees you seven years' bad luck and a lot of grief from your left-handed spouse who's equally superstitious about anything dealing with the Right Wing.

Deciding who gets which side of the bed is a major marital challenge that should not be taken lightly. Why do you think months of time, energy, and expense were expended on selecting new sheets, pillowcases, bed skirts, pillow shams, duvets, bedspreads, and that potpourri stuff in the dish on the nightstand that is nothing but a blatant fire hazard? It wasn't so you could sleep. It was so you could stay up until the wee hours of the morning arguing about who gets which side of the bed! Don't get me started about feather versus foam pillows.

Middle-of-the-Bed Fred. This mattress malady speaks for itself. I hate to be the bearer of bad bed news, but once you do reach a mutually satisfactory agreement on who gets which side of the bed, that won't resolve anything. It doesn't matter if you and your hubby sleep in a twin-, queen-, or king-sized bed, your Middle-of-the-Bed Fred will soon be dead if he doesn't change his bed-hogging ways. Not a great way to start life together. Typically, a Middle-of-the-Bed Fred was raised as a precocious only child of overindulgent parents, which explains his Space Dominance Syndrome. He always got his way and his space and has never once been put in his place. If Fred isn't an only brat, I mean, child, then your snoozing centrist probably comes from a large family of eight or more kids. Forced to share a bed with at least two other siblings for the first eighteen years of his life, you've inherited a bed-consuming Andean condor who never got the chance to spread his wings.

The only effective way to deal with a Middle-of-the-Bed Fred is to make a significant financial investment in one of those large surgical tables used by veterinarians for operating on wildebeests or hippos. Now I do admit that this may seem a bit bizarre and financially unfeasible for couples who are trying to save money for a down payment on a new home. But, in order to move Middle-of-the-Bed Fred's big derriere, you are going to need this specialized table, which comes equipped with a horizontally tilting hydraulic lift. The second Middle-of-the-Bed Fred begins his anatomical encroachment onto your side of the bed, all you have to do is simply flip a switch, the bed will tilt, and Middle-of-the-Bed Fred will flop over to his side like a Filet-o'-Fish sandwich.

So, instead of your getting packed like a salted sardine into one-sixteenth of the bed, Fred gets put in his proper place, and you get your beauty rest. If you think Middle-of-the-Bed Fred will balk at the cost, you can sell him on the hydraulic lift extension kit, which is exactly like the ones used in auto-repair shops. You'll be able to get your sleep, and he'll be able to tune up his car. The thousands of dollars you'll save on auto repair and the lost hours of productivity from sleep deprivation will soon add up to a nice, fat down payment for your dream home.

The Whacker: Let me be very clear. I am not an advocate of spousal violence. But, in some cases, it is okay to slug your spouse back if he or she whacks you while asleep in bed. I already know what some of you engaged people are thinking: *Yeah right! My husband or wife is going to hit me when I'm asleep? You think I'm that bad a judge of character?* Go ahead. I once thought the same thing until I got Whacker dental work. For those newlyweds out there, you're on my side. You know exactly what I'm talking about.

We say, "Beware of the Whacker."

Whacking is a very real phenomenon experienced by newlyweds worldwide. A newlywed Whacker is a spouse who karate-chops you while you're both asleep. A Whacker typically has guillotine arms, hair-trigger elbows, and legs that kick like mules ready to be emasculated. Sounds strange, I know, but newlywed Whackers can cause severe physical harm for innocent spouses who do not wear hockey goalie gear to bed.

When you first get whacked by your newlywed Whacker, it'll scare the snot outta you because you'll think you're being attacked by a cat burglar or your local serial killer.

KAA-WHAM!

"Uumph! Aahhh! What are you doing?"

Silence.

The Whacker is still asleep.

He doesn't even know that he just broke your nose.

As you lie weeping in bed, moaning over your injuries, the Whacker will autonomically reload during the REM cycle. Then, when you sit down to breakfast the next morning and your Whacker says to you over poached eggs the size of your swollen lips and coffee as black as your left eye, "Gee, honey, whadya do? Fall outta bed?" you'll begin to see the seriousness of this violent sleep disorder.

When the Whacker will whack again is difficult to predict, primarily because of changes in his or her sleeping position as well as changes in your own sleeping position. Just think how many near misses you've already had and don't even know about. Last week, it was a donkey kick to your groin. What's it going to be this week? An elbow in the eye? Five flanges in the face?

To remedy the wild ways of a newlywed Whacker, simply purchase the same feet-and-ankle cuffs used to transport prisoners. Sounds kinda kinky, I know, but don't get the wrong idea. Don't allow your marriage to be put into bondage by a newlywed Whacker. Your personal safety is at stake, and if the Whacker is properly restrained when he or she strikes again, the only damage will be caused by and to the Whacker. Self-inflicted whacking is the sole way to whack sense into a Whacker.

TOGETHER FOREVER

Deciding who gets which side of the bed, dealing with a Middle-of-the-Bed Fred, or defending yourself against a newlywed Whacker are all considerable challenges, but they aren't insurmountable challenges if you have a healthy sense of humor. What many young married couples don't find very funny, though, is how truly challenging married life can really be. If marriage were as simple and easy as changing your name on your personal checks, driver's license, social-security account, and any other important business information, would there be so many unhappy marriages? I don't think so.

Marriage is filled with many challenges that happen within the relationship and from the world outside of the relationship, and one of the chief tasks newly married couples have to brace themselves for is the challenge to be challenged.

Did you hear me closely? Prepare to be challenged.

Marriage means you will be challenged like never before.

Last summer, I was invited to speak to a weeklong high-school summer camp in the San Bernardino Mountains. Since Krista was eight months' pregnant with our fourth child, she preferred to stay home and sleep in the comfort of her own bed, rather than sleeping on a hard bunk with a twenty-year-old mattress shaped like a skateboard half-pipe. Dining on a week's worth of sloppy joes, spaghetti, and who-knows-what-kind-of-rodent-they-lured-into-the-kitchen-tonight didn't thrill her either, so Krista stayed home with our three kids while I hung out with high-school students. That, for me, was a challenge. Not hanging out with kids, but being away from my family. Whenever I'm away from home, I have trouble sleeping. It's easy to spend night after night tossing and turning, wondering when in the world I am going to fall asleep. I get lonely. I miss Krista. I miss my kids' hugs and kisses. I miss my home.

On this particular trip, I learned something new that has helped me look at my life and my marriage in a new way. One afternoon I went to the camp's "motivational challenge course," where they instill in you a fervent belief in God and the afterlife by having you climb up a fifty-foot tree stump to stand on a tiny, two-foot platform and then screaming at you until you leap for a hanging trapeze out of arm's reach as if you were the Great Asti Spumante. Challenge courses have all sorts of other sick contraptions like zip lines, climbing walls, and tightropes designed to help you wrestle with one of life's most perplexing questions, "Why in the world did I let myself get talked into doing *THIS?*"

As I walked around watching high-school students laugh and scream and cheer each other on at the various stations, one particular act caught my eye. As the challenge course instructor tied a student's harness and gave a final word of encouragement, before any student was allowed to begin the course, each had to say their name and the following words:

My name is Tony, and I accept this challenge.

My name is Susan, and I accept this challenge.

My name is Jake, and I accept this challenge.

The climbing wall. The zip line. The high ropes. The low ropes. The spine adjuster. The barfomatic. The you-are-no-longer-sixteen-years-old. The I-can't-go-home-injured-and-have-my-wife-say-I-told-you-so. Each station I went to, I heard the same words over and over again.

My name is _______, and I accept this challenge.

Don't you think that these same words repeated over and over again by high-school students on the challenge course should be how you and I approach our marriages every day of our lives? I have no idea what kinds of challenges you are facing in your marriage right now or what kinds of challenges you will face together in the future, but I do know that in order to have your wedding cake and eat it too, to live a happily married life in which you both enjoy growing old together forever, you have to be willing to take on each day with an attitude that accepts challenges as a permanent reality in daily life.

What challenge is your marriage facing right now? Are you getting on each other's nerves like a couple of high-school students scratching their nails on a chalkboard? Are you feeling a bit overwhelmed by this marriage thing and not sure if you can make it for the long haul? Are your in-laws driving you bonkers? Do you ever wonder why you married an inconsiderate, nasty mongoose of a mate who used to be the nicest, most considerate person in the world? Did you think this sex thing would be a snap and discover that it is anything but that? Do you argue about roles and who should do what when because you did it last week? Are you struggling with finances and wondering why in the world your spouse doesn't handle money like you? Is your most frequent form of communication fighting? Do you have a sick family member or pressures at work? Do some of your friends treat you differently now that you're married? Do you spend less fun and romantic time together now than you did when you were dating? Do you feel like your spouse is your number one challenge and you are the challengee? Are you feeling challenged instead of feeling chosen?

If you picked one item in the previous list, then you have a normal marriage. If you picked three to five items, you have a normal marriage. If you picked all of the above items and added about ten more to your growing list, then, yes, you, too, have a normal marriage. Challenges are the norm of married life. You cannot be married and not face difficult marital challenges any more than you can be single and not face the challenges presented in being single. You were born on a planet that is one huge challenge course. What your marriage and every marriage needs is two people committed to supporting one another through the challenges of married life and the challenges that the world throws at them. Every day of married life, one of your primary responsibilities and commitments is to support your spouse with whatever challenge your marriage faces. Living on the ropes course that we do, there is just no other way to have your cake and eat it too.

When you're struggling with a difficult challenge in your marriage, the Bible tells you and your spouse to "bear with each other" (Col. 3:13). You help carry each other's loads. If your husband is standing fifty feet off the deck and is scared to jump, you cheer him on! If your wife is frozen to the climbing wall like a Popsicle stuck to a frozen waterfall, you scream your support! If you and your spouse are tied onto the same rope on the high ropes wondering why in the world you ever got married, you look at each other straight in the eye and say with wild abandon, "C'mon! We can do this!"

Instead of ripping each other up like two grizzlies fighting over a salmon steak, you support, encourage, listen, confront, forgive, and work toward resolving the differences you have or the problems confronting your marriage from the world outside. Bearing with each other and supporting each other doesn't mean you'll lose every argument. It doesn't mean you'll win every argument either. It doesn't guarantee victory or doom you to defeat. What it does mean is that there is far more value in supporting one another than getting one up on your spouse. Whatever challenge you face, if you support one another, you both win.

We all need a challenge, but we can't do it without support. Marriage presents plenty of challenging opportunities to learn more about ourselves and more about one another. Being willing to face your challenges together and supporting one another in the process is what enables you to have your cake and eat it too because the husbands and wives who support each other through the good times and the bad are the same ones who stay together forever.

The ultimate challenge for marriage, then, is to recite a very simple statement every day for the rest of your life:

My name is ________, and I accept this challenge.

Go ahead and sign your name.

I dare you.

FOR NEARLYWEDS

What has been the most challenging aspect of your engagement so far? What challenges do you foresee in married life? How do you support each other in tough times?

FOR NEWLYWEDS

What has been the biggest challenge in your marriage so far? Too often we give support in the way we'd like to receive it. Right now, think about a particular challenge you've faced in your marriage and write down two or three ways you think your spouse would like your support. Now go ask him or her. Find out exactly how your spouse would like to be supported and see what difference it makes in your marriage.

Your Mother-in-Law's Guide to Marriage

15

I'm surprised my mother-in-law isn't nicer to me.
With the kind of husband her son made,
you'd think she'd be afraid I'd sue her.
—Phyllis Diller

I don't understand why everyone is so down on mothers-in-law.

I think every inmate should have one.

At practically every rehearsal dinner I've ever been to, when it comes time to making toasts and roasts, the parents of the bride and groom get up and say the same thing that is being said at every rehearsal dinner that night across the country. A teary-eyed dad stands up and says in a choked up voice, "Ever since Bobby, sorry, Robert was a little baby, Marge and I have prayed for a special little lady to come into his life and become his wife. We are so pleased that our prayers have been answered in such a wonderful young lady like Jennifer. We not only have a fine son, but we're also receiving a new daughter. Marge and I would like to welcome you to the family, Jennifer."

Polite applause from the bridal party.

That was dear old dad talking.

Standing next to her blubbering, bleeding-heart husband, future mother-in-law Marge is thinking the polar opposite.[1] What

[1] Author's note: The following characterization represents Marge, not all mothers-in-law. Especially those living in North America and those related to the person reading this book at this very moment.

Marge really wants to do is grab the microphone and give this whiny son-stealer what she's got coming to her. Marge fantasizes locking the Louis Vuitton designer daughter-in-law in her cold, dingy basement for a weekend of Bobby Reeducation Boot Camp so this little missy doesn't mess up the twenty-five years she spent slaving to perfect her son.

An evil, sinister smile crinkles across Marge's upper lip, where a mole the size of a Milk Dud with three black hairs is sticking out of it, which the waiters across the room point at when Marge is not looking. As the toasting, laughter, and merriment of the rehearsal dinner flows like the champagne refills, Marge gurgles a throaty, raspy chuckle and envisions a weekend alone in the bellows of her basement with her little pet.

"A bit of sleep deprivation, a little mental manipulation, some electrical stimulation, and Jen-ni-fer will be mine, ALL MINE!"

Jennifer cowers in a corner, wondering how the basement door got locked.

"All right, JEN-NI-FER! You're going to listen and listen good. Ever since the day Bobby was born, I've steeled my mind for this magical moment. Since you have managed to woo and win my one and only son away from me, I don't want you to consider me your mother-in-law, and I don't want you to consider yourself my daughter-in-law. I have no daughters! Only a son, who in two days' time will be poisoned, weakened, and broken by your soft, slithery, and slippery feminine touch. No, we are not in-laws . . . consider us *partners.* I will be your mentor, and you will be my protégée in protecting what I have spent the past twenty-five years perfecting . . ."

Jennifer attempts to peep, "But—"

Marge grabs a nearby cattle prod and screams, "SILENCE! You will do as I say and say as I do. You will not speak unless told to speak. Is that understood?"

Jennifer nods, wishing she would have never broken up with Trent Lockheart in eleventh grade.

"Bobby, you see, is a special boy. There's never been another boy like my Bobby, and there never will be. Bobby's lips have never tasted processed food. His clothes have always been neatly starched and pressed. He shares my love for classical music, even though he says he hates it. He had never seen an R-rated movie until you came along. He wrote to me every week when he was in college. Bobby understands obedience, order, and discipline, and you will do nothing to countermand the regimen I have established for his life. Under my strict leadership and training, I expect, no, I demand that you seek my counsel before making any decision that pertains to Bobby's well-being. As the two of you prepare to procreate to ensure the pedigree of our lineage, I will provide further instruction concerning proper consummation techniques and positions."

Cowering in fear, Jennifer slides her engagement ring off her finger. "Here, you can have it back."

Marge sneers and throws her head back in mad laughter. "You're not getting off that easy, my little pretty! We're partners now! Welcome to the Snodgrass family!"

Okay, so maybe all mothers-in-law are not that demented. *Maybe.* Still, behind every wedding toast are a host of silent, unwritten, unspoken laws that are perpetuated by the pantheon of past mothers-in-law. Whether you are the bride or groom, here is the unofficial Mother-in-Law's Guide to Marriage.

YOUR MOTHER-IN-LAW'S GUIDE TO MARRIAGE

Everything you know about marriage is wrong.
I know everything there is to know about marriage.
You are responsible for my child's complete happiness.
If you mistreat my child in any way, I will break you.
My child is perfect. He/she can do no wrong.
We have a happy, well-adjusted family.
You came from a dysfunctional family.

If a conflict arises between my child and you,
don't ask whose side I'm on.
Challenge me, and you will regret it for the rest of your life.
My opinion matters. I will give it unsolicited.
If guilt doesn't work, I will resort to painful measures.
Move away and you can expect two-week visits at random.
You will bear me grandchildren.
If you are unable to have children, the bad gene is on your side.
You know nothing about parenting.
Your children are mine.
I helped you with a down payment on your home.
Su casa es mi casa.
I will show up unannounced.
I will stay for dinner and for as long as I please.
Our family has top priority for all holidays.
We do not have a will.
We have a trust in our child's name.
You will push my wheelchair with a smile on your face.
Groveling is good for the soul.

For all the brouhaha made about bad mothers-in-law, nothing can compare to the tumultuous, stomach-acid-producing task of when a guy has to ask his girlfriend's father for her hand in marriage. This is where we clearly delineate the men from the boys, the winners from the wusses, the leaders from the losers, the studs from the slugs, and the heroic from the hairballs.

There are two types of future grooms.

The grooms with guts.

The grooms without guts.

Guys (capital *G* for greatness, denoting strength and power) who ask.

guys (small *g* for gutlessness, denoting mushroom spores and single-cell amoebae) who don't ask.

The guys (small *g*) who are afraid to go man to man with The Main Man are the ones who put off the engagement until a big family event like Christmas or Fourth of July when they will find strength in family numbers. When they pop the question, these handball-against-the-curb players think that if they just buy a big enough ring, then they'll be able to hide behind the glistening rock on their fiancée's finger. Then, when a hundred or so people are gathered in the living room, this brave, courageous turnip will make his bold proclamation.

"Ann and I would like to make a very important announcement . . ."

Next to Uncle Charlie stands Mr. Jones, Ann's father. Mr. Jones is in a fun and festive mood. He's holding a gin and tonic.

"Today, I asked Ann to marry me . . ."

Mr. Jones's face contorts into a blood-red boil as he squeezes his drink.

". . . and she said yes!"

The distinctive popping sound of breaking glass shatters the silence but is quickly muffled by the roar of cheering relatives.

Whether or not to ask a father for his daughter's hand in marriage is just a question of pain now or pain later. Real Guys (big *G*) deal with the pain up front because asking her father is going to be a whole lot harder than asking her. There's nothing that strikes fear into the heart of guys more than approaching two hands holding up a newspaper on the living-room sofa.

"Um, Mr. Jones?"

"Humph."

"Uh, sir, there's something I'd like to speak to you about."

"Humph. Pass me the sports page, will ya?"

"Yes sir. Ann and I are tired of being free agents, you know?"

"Geez, Dodgers lost again. Hand me the business section."

"What we're talking about, Mr. Jones, sir, is a major merger and acquisition that will deal a significant financial blow to your pocketbook."

"Ah, IBM's down two and a quarter. Give me the movie guide."

"Ann and I, you could say, are ready to make our own motion picture."

"Harrumph. Nothing good's playing. Whaddya say we watch some TV?"

"Yes sir."

Once a dad finally clues in that his future son-in-law is talking about marrying *his daughter,* the first questions we know for sure are racing through Dad's mind are those of a sexual nature: "Did you have sex with my daughter? Did you touch her in any unclean way? Did you impregnate her?" Then comes the two-hour interview during which Dad relishes in making his future son-in-law squirm and grovel and provide him with the last three years' tax returns, credit history, two official forms of identification, complete medical records, driving record, church affiliation, proof of U.S. citizenship, political leanings, notable awards and achievements, family planning plans, and direct lineage tracing back to the Mayflower or at least as far back as the signing of the Louisiana Purchase.

That's for the two-hour interview.

When I asked Krista to marry me, her dad and I had a little chat for *three hours.*

TOGETHER FOREVER

I have absolutely no idea what kind of family you're marrying into. And neither do you. I mean, you may have a pretty good idea of what your new husband's or wife's family is like before you get married. You could be marrying into the Hugger Family, where everyone is into group hugs, bear hugs, backslapping hugs, touchy-feely hugs, ad nauseam, ad infinitum. Or maybe you're getting hitched to the Quiet Family, and you come from the Loud Family. This, I guarantee you, will drive you crazy during holidays and family dinners where the only sounds heard at the table are clinking silverware and soft whispers of "Please pass the imitation crab salad." Coming from the Loud Family, everyone in your family shouted and hooted and hollered at the dinner table as if you sat at the end of a 747 runway for every meal. Then there's the Mystery Family, where everyone talks in code, and you're almost positive there are more skeletons in the closet than the average-sized cemetery of a major metropolitan city. You could have jumped into the Twelve-Step Family, where everyone's in recovery and if you're not, it's because you're still in denial. You might marry into the Happy Family, where everyone smiles so much it makes your face hurt. Or you just may marry into the Average American Family where everyone is, well, average.

No matter how well you think you know what kind of family you're marrying into or how much your spouse's family influenced your decision to get married, in-law relations are a major part of married life. Marriage makes you family, so it's critically important to know how to get along with your in-laws so your marriage will benefit from the positive outcomes of healthy family relationships. Having your wedding cake and eating it too means learning how to manage extended family matters in a way that's beneficial for as many family members as possible.

Marriage First, Family Second. The moment you and your immortal beloved were pronounced husband and wife, you became one in spirit and purpose. Though you both have individual personalities, preferences, likes and dislikes, needs and desires, God has made you one as a couple. The marriage bed is where you became one flesh, and that's where you'll conceive a family of your own. (Locations may vary.) You have both left your mothers and fathers to start a life of your own.

You are now one.

There is only one, hear me, *one couple* on top of a wedding cake.

Not four. Not eight. Not fifty-five, including second cousins thrice removed.

You and your mate are one, and that's the way God intended it to be.

Your challenge as husband and wife is to develop your own separate identity as a couple and as a family. Therefore, your marriage and everything pertaining to married life comes first, and your extended family comes second. The tug of family loyalty can be a powerful pull when you're trying to figure out how to start your new life together. One of the most common newlywed conflicts you'll go through is when your in-laws come between you and your spouse. Your parents or your spouse's parents may jump into one of your conflicts uninvited. Or you or your spouse may run to dear old Mom or Dad for help without first trying to solve the problem together. If you or your spouse allow each other's in-laws to come between the two of you, it's going to get pretty crowded on top of that wedding cake. To have your wedding cake and eat it too, you have to be committed to the idea of Oneness. Make your marriage first and your family second.

Establish Boundaries. Some parents have helped their kids all their lives, so when precious little Bobby, sorry, Robert gets married, they just don't know how to stop helping. Knowing when to say no and knowing when to say yes to in-laws is one of the trickiest struggles for newly married couples. Many newlyweds have problems with one of the shortest words in the English language: *no*.

Developing a sense of marriage independence apart from the input and influence from your family isn't an easy thing to do. The family you came from is familiar, comfortable, and predictable. For many newlyweds, the first year or two of marriage is anything but familiar, comfortable, and predictable. As a new husband or wife, you have to continually ask yourself, *Who is my first loyalty to?*

One of the best conversations you can have with one another during your engagement and your first couple of years of marriage is deciding when to tell your parents yes and when to say no. Practice saying it in the mirror if you have to. *No* isn't negative if you're saying yes to a decision that ultimately helps your marriage grow.

Withhold a Critical Spirit. When there's conflict in your extended families, whether you're warring with your in-laws or your wife is ready to give Marge a little cattle-prod motivation to get out of the house, use good judgment in handling the problem, and if at all possible, withhold a critical spirit toward whoever is causing the conflict. There is no perfect family. Some families are a lot more complicated than others, but don't let your best energy and enthusiasm for your marriage get drained by in-law conflicts. Though you may not understand why your spouse's family are distant relatives to the Addams family, take the high road and refuse to be critical. Don't let someone else's thoughtless words, attitudes, or actions poison your spirit and your marriage. You cannot control what your in-laws do, but you can control how you respond to them. As husband and wife, pay attention to how extended family conflicts can drain your love for one another.

Be Willing to Take Advice. Your in-laws can be a great source of help, encouragement, and support in your first few years of marriage and in many years to come. Whatever family you marry into, remember that in-laws can teach you a lot about marriage, a lot about raising a family, a lot about God and other people, a lot about finances and good decision making, and a lot about life in general.

You and your spouse will benefit by being teachable and flexible in how you relate to your in-laws. Many in-laws are tremendous sources of wisdom, knowledge, and experience. What parent doesn't want good things for their sons and daughters? By staying open to new ideas and input, when it's appropriate, you and your spouse can save yourselves years of frustration and hassles that come from poor decision making made from inexperience or impulsiveness.

And that's a better motivator than a cattle prod.

FOR NEARLYWEDS

Pick a funny term to describe your family. Talk about your own family's strengths and weaknesses. (Not your fiancée's family.) What are important things you should know about each other's family before you get married?

FOR NEWLYWEDS

In the past year or so, how have your in-laws been sources of help or encouragement? How have they not? Why is it so critical to have your own separate identity as a married couple? What is one area in which you need to learn to say no to your in-laws? What is one area in which you need to learn to say yes to your in-laws in terms of what you can learn from them?

Your Bride Has Arachnophobia

16

There are certain jobs, for all her liberation, she will not do. She doesn't refuse to do them; it simply never occurs to her that she might actually change a light bulb. Or empty the trash compactor. If she sees an insect, she traps it under a glass until I get home.

—Tom, Washington, D.C.

When I asked Krista to marry me and she said yes, my first response was elation. After a blink or two, my second response was utter amazement. Wide-eyed in wonder, adrenaline-laced brain fuel flushed over my mental afterburners. "She didn't balk. Didn't hesitate a second. Didn't flinch an inch. No deer-in-the-headlights, frozen Cindy-Brady face staring at the quiz-show TV cameras. She wants to spend the rest of her life with me?! This woman has no fear!"

No fear, I marveled. *This is one brave woman.*

All that changed the day we got married.

During our engagement, Krista had carefully constructed a silky, enticing web of honeymoon hunger to hide a horrible, heinous secret. She drew me like the innocent male black widow wanting to mate into her icky-sticky web of deceit until I was so entangled in her love that there was no possible chance of escape.

Before we got married, how was I supposed to know she had an irrational, I mean, insightful perspective on all things creepy-crawly? How was I supposed to know this psychological spider disorder dated all the way back to kindergarten, when she refused to sing "The Itsy-Bitsy Spider"? How was I supposed to know that *engagement* and *extermination* were synonyms? How was I supposed to know that Krista had a severe case of arachnophobia? We're talking *Psycho*-screams-in-the-shower arachnophobia. When we stood at the altar and the preacher told me to kiss my bride, how was I supposed to know that what I was really getting was *The Kiss of the Spider Woman*?

Krista's aversion for all nonhuman life forms includes every spider great and small, adamant ants, menacing mice, slithering silverfish, terrifying termites drunk on dry rot, loathsome earwigs with waists that wiggle like toy hula dolls on dashboards, wasps with attitude problems, blood-sucking vampire cockroaches that scurry from kitchen lights at three in the morning, any mammal classified as a rodent (husbands occasionally included), harmless Jiminy Crickets, fearless flies (which includes their legless, soft-bodied pupae stage, i.e., maggots), unidentifiable black bugs in Captain Crunch cereal boxes, ticked off fleas who've contracted Rocky Mountain spotted fever from ticks, any unexplainable itching that can be blamed on microscopic mites, dead bugs in cobwebby corners, rigor mortis mice caught in thumb-snapping, why-don't-you-set-your-own mousetraps, or any rhinoceros beetles found in safari outfits on the dirty clothes pile.

After our wedding, I wasn't out of my tuxedo for two seconds, wasn't even the man of the house for a minute, when I became the Orkin Man. I went from being a fiancé to being a fumigator. When I tried to carry her across the threshold, Krista raised her Black Flag and refused to enter my roach motel. She waited out on the front porch while I lured the cockroaches in our condominium out with half a bean-and-cheese burrito. The poor suckers didn't even have a chance to scream "Raid!" before I blasted 'em with a lethal dose of dimethylcyclopropanecarboxylic acid and a dash of tetrabromoethyl.

So now I am the only guy in my neighborhood who wears a bug beeper.

I am on a twenty-four-hour radio alert to meet my wife's entomology needs.

Our home is a rodent-free zone.

We're the only family in our neighborhood with its own termite tent.

We even have a bumper sticker on our car that says, "Bug Abuse Is Life Abuse." So, I don't abuse bugs. I kill them with Ortho kindness.

Now that I think about it, we could have nipped this arachnophobia problem like an aphid in a rosebud during premarital counseling. Nobody even thought to ask Krista or me the simple question, "What do you fear?" Maybe we could have been asked a more general, less threatening question like, "What really bugs you?" Our premarital counselor could have at least provided us some sort of psychological phobia profile, a simple checklist on a clipboard like in a physician's office, where we could jot down what scares us or bugs us.

Do I have to do everything here? A simple checklist was all that was needed. Wasn't there anyone else who could have come up with something like this years ago? A simple tool like this that could have saved thousands of marriages from getting bitten by the arachnophobia bug that has plagued Orkin mankind since the bubonic Black Death of the Middle Ages? To be forewarned is to be forearmed, so I have taken the liberty to help all guykind, the Future Fumigators of America, to kill on contact any secret infestation fears with the following arachnophobia checklist.

Talk about building the perfect mousetrap.

Well, here it is! Welcome to holy arachnidmony.

ARACHNOPHOBIA CHECKLIST

Please check the following items that make you jump, squirm, shriek, screech, scream, run, flee, vacate, or call on any male within three square miles for assistance:

____ Spider not bothering anyone
____ Spider on bedspread
____ Big spider lands on hand
____ Ant (1)
____ Ants covering the trash and sink
____ Ants stealing your new fondue pot
____ Cockroach (1)
____ Cockroaches (2–100)
____ Cockroaches with AK-47s
____ Angry wasps
____ Wasps on PCP
____ Wasps in Walkmans
____ Silverfish in books
____ Silverfish in salads
____ Silverfish in sleepwear
____ Circus flea
____ Flesh-hungry flea
____ Billowing, black cloud of fleas
____ Mouse
____ Stuart Little
____ Mickey Mouse
____ Disease-carrying rodent
____ Nice rat (cleans up after itself)
____ Fat rat
____ Rat bigger than your bullmastiff

How I wish I would have had an arachnophobia checklist before I got married! I'm usually not in favor of prenuptial agreements, but I'm also no advocate of arachnophobic wives who can't kill a spider for themselves. I mean, what if I had been a closet bug pacifist? Krista and I could have made the "Weddings and Engagements" section of the *National Enquirer.* Can't you imagine the headline?

Bug Pacifist Marries Arachnophobic: No Shrill Can Make Him Kill!

It has all the makings of a Greek tragedy or an edgy Jane Austen thriller.

Over the years, I resigned myself to the fact that if I want to be a real man in my wife's eyes, then I need to be the Orkin Man. To silence her screams, I really don't mind the occasional task of grabbing a Kleenex and crushing an innocent spider right in its cephalothorax, though after the third trip to the hospital for getting jumped by a resilient gang of black widows hiding behind her hutch, I do think I deserve a set of bug-proof body armor.

I do have to say that killing spiders isn't too bad, but what really bugs me are ants.

Ask my wife. I'm on an ant rant.

Do I look like one big aphid or what?

For the past two months, I kid you not, our home has turned into a veritable ant colony. The queen has taken up residence somewhere within the walls of our home, and she is waging guerrilla warfare. I'm so battle weary from so many ant attacks that I am ready to go ballistic next time I see a line of scouts snaking up our walls or sneaking out of an electric socket or lugging a load of tuna fish across the carpet for a late-night colony snack.

Ants are in my office. In my desk. In our kids' rooms. In the family room. The kitchen. Under the sink. In the trash. In the cupboards. Loping down the hallway with our leftovers, these stinking ants are everywhere! Krista finally gave me one of those ant hotels that are supposed to attract the ants with poisonous food that will be carried back to feed the queen. I put the dang thing in my desk drawer, thinking, *Yeah, this'll kill 'em!* I came back a few hours later, and I had more ants in my desk drawer than words in this book. The little buggers were screaming to their amigos crawling out from the nearby light socket, "Dude, the party's up here in the desk drawer! It's another one of those dumb food traps that makes us multiply even quicker!"

Our friends come over and comment on our moving walls.

"Ants? Those aren't ants," I protest with embarrassment impossible to hide. "It's Spanish Mission wall art. Goes back to the early California days of Father Serra Junípero ."

In the past eight weeks, I have killed at least ten million ants, but these insipid little buggers keep on coming. I spray. I set ant traps with poison bait. It's gotten so bad, I'm even breaking all sorts of laws. I violate federal laws by using antiant products in a manner inconsistent with their labeling. I do not "shake well before using." I shake with rage. I do not store my cans of Raid Ant and Roach Killer in a cool, dry place. I use the ant spray as a room spray, an air freshener of sorts. I do not mix two teaspoons of Ortho concentrate per gallon of water; I mix two gallons of Ortho concentrate per *teaspoon* of water. (If the EPA hasn't got a better idea, then phooey on them!) I do not spray ants from an eight-to twelve-inch distance. I kill 'em on contact by getting right up to their insipid, insectoid pointers and spraying 'em like a pesticide fire hose. It's gotta burn their tiny little eyes . . . *Ah-hah-hah-hah-hah!* I create my own bug bombs by making Molotov cocktails with my Raid cans. I puncture the aerosol container with a screwdriver, light a match, and *kawhooosh!* the whole kit and caboodle gets thrown at the fire ants in my home office. Let 'em all burn! I may not finish my book, but I don't care anymore!

Hey, I'm desperate. You would be too if your manhood was on the line.

If Krista has to call a professional exterminator, what will that make me?

I went from being a fiancé to a fumigator . . . what else do I know?

TOGETHER FOREVER

Not all women have an arachnid aversion. I've actually known a few guys who've gotten in fights over carefully placed earwigs in sleeping bags. I don't know who the amateur exterminator is in your household, but once you get married, an amazing thing happens. It's the same thing that happens to every newlywed couple: You go from being bugged by bugs to bugging one another. You go from saying, "Spiders bug me" to giving your husband or wife the evil stink eye and saying, "You bug me!"

When your spouse begins to bug you or when you start to bug your spouse is not a matter of "if." It's only a matter of "when." It could happen when your husband tosses a sand crab on your towel when you're honeymooning in Hawaii, or it could happen when you're trying to agree on the color and shape of soap for the soap dish in your first few weeks of marriage, or it could happen a year or two after you've been married and it finally dawns on you one day that marriage does not give your husband the right to pick his nose in the car or in front of your parents.

When your husband or wife is bugging the heck out of you, this is known in extermination trade parlance as a "Relational Infestation Fight," or a RIF. Common English usage for this term is heard in such statements as "My wife and I are having a major RIF," or "Could you please put down that can of Raid? I don't have time for such a childish RIF," or "You really RIF me off!"

Most RIFs could be altogether avoided or seriously toned down if newly married couples had an accurate checklist of the annoying actions, disgusting habits, irky quirks, weird idiosyncrasies, and bugging behaviors that spawn newlywed RIFs. Like the much-needed premarital Arachnophobia Checklist, there's an even stronger need for identifying bothersome bride behaviors and disgusting groom gross-outs before the RIFs start to swarm. Sooner or later, every newlywed couple is going to get RIFed about something the other person does or says. You can tell your spouse is a household pest when . . .

Wife boldly belches Beethoven's Fifth in public and laughs with glee.	Husband belches, and he's the most disgusting thing on two legs.
Wife steals hubby's razor. Shaves legs in sink. Leaves stubble for hubby to clean.	Hubby shaves, adding to wife's razor gunk. Husband gets blamed for not cleaning sink.
Wife goes to video store for a movie they "both can watch" and rents a chick flick.	Husband rents any video with explosions, machine guns, or a sexy girl on the cover.
Husband gives wife helpful advice, but wife doesn't listen.	Her mother tells her the exact same thing and wife thinks her mom is brilliant.
Wife agrees to the new annual budget subject to the terms and conditions set forth by Visa, MasterCard, or American Express.	Husband always has a logical, rational justification for his purchases at the expense of the new annual budget.
Wife vehemently insists utensils be placed "up" in the dishwasher.	Husband places utensils "down" in dishwasher and runs it two or three times or until utensils are clean.
Wife is anal about how the bed is made.	Husband has never made a bed.
Wife doesn't keep the refrigerator adequately stocked like Mom did.	Husband puts juice pitcher back in fridge with one fluid ounce remaining so he doesn't have to clean it out.
Wife insists that expensive manicures and pedicures are good hygiene.	Husband picks toenails on bed and throws scraps on carpet. Refuses to use clippers.
Wife sets annual calendar around Twice-Yearly sale at Nordstrom and any outlet mall within one hundred square miles. Catalog shopping does not count as real shopping.	Husband sets annual calendar around the four major seasons: baseball season, basketball season, football season, and hunting season.
Wife pokes and jabs husband with sharp fingernail to stop his snoring. Jabs draw blood.	Husband steals covers from wife and denies said behavior.
Wife poofs in bed, laughs, and says, "It was only a little one."	Husband poofs in bed, grunts, and says, "Whoever smelt it, dealt it."

If your husband or wife is bugging you, or if you're bugged by the fact that your spouse gets bugged by something that seems like no big deal to you, you can be sure you're not alone. We all do things that bug our husband or wife. The first year of marriage can be very unsettling when you discover that your perfect mate is one big nematode. If you feel like you're getting on each other's nerves and the frosting on your wedding cake is tasting a little sour, here are a few things to think about before grabbing the fly swatter.

Is It Worth Raising a Stink? Long before you and your spouse were married, you each developed unique habits, tastes, likes and dislikes, preferences, and ways of thinking. Whatever habit you find most annoying, don't be too surprised when you discover your spouse has an affinity for that particular habit. Though your husband or wife may do something on the level of a stink bug, ask yourself if you want to raise a stink over this issue. Too often, a bugged and bothered spouse will try to change the annoying spouse by getting in their face like a pesky gnat. Don't allow your husband's or wife's bad habit to get you in the habit of bugging them to death. It's fine to make your irritation known to the mosquito you married, but if you keep scratching at the bite, the problem's only going to swell. Which is greater: the problem itself or your reaction to the problem?

Dissect the Problem, Not the Person. Say your husband does something that really bugs you, like never calling when he's going to be home late or exhibiting symptoms of Honey-Do ADD. (He always doesn't do what he says he's going to do.) When your husband has miraculously lowered himself from a knight in shining armor to a horned toad who wants something for nothing, it's very easy to want to pin him down like your belligerent bullfrog in Biology 101 and dissect his innards. A lot of first-year fights and irritations are the result of a lot of near misses: misunderstandings, mistaken assumptions, and miscommunications. Whether it's your husband or wife who's bugging you, nobody likes being put under a microscope. Instead of dissecting your spouse, you need to dissect the problem. Don't make the mistake of making what bugs you into a major character issue that your spouse needs to change. Instead of trying to change your spouse, be willing to separate the problem from the person you married by refusing to react and, instead, waiting for an opportune time to talk about working on the problem together. You married a person, not a problem. Which one do you want to attack?

Practice Patience. Patience is a character quality that you cannot do without in marriage. When your spouse is bugging you, patience is the frosting on the cake that can keep you from losing your cool. Patience is an essential character quality you want to wear like a thick overcoat in your marriage. Some of the minor irritants, distractions, and newly married annoyances just aren't worth fighting over. Practicing patience, the art of self-control in how you respond with your words and actions, can mean the difference between a blowup and a better way of understanding the person you married.

Just because you bug your husband or your husband bugs you doesn't mean you don't love each other. Bugging behavior is a sign that you are both unique individuals. To get past the flytraps of bitterness or unkind words, you both need to practice patience in those things that enter at your fingernails, crawl underneath your skin, and jump on your nerves like dive-bombing kamikaze mosquitoes. Practicing patience builds strength and endurance in your life and in marriage. A quality marriage isn't built by easy times; it's built by times of testing, frustration, and conflict, which, when those conflicts are worked through, produce strength and endurance for the long haul.

Patience enables you and me to have our cake and eat it too by not having a hair trigger on the spray can of spousal annoyances. I readily admit I could use more patience in my own life. When waging war by myself against a fierce ant attack larger than the Russian army, I've blown my cool plenty of times by screaming in a fit of self-pity, "How come I'm the only one around here killing all these stinking ants!"

But I know practicing patience is good for my marriage.

I am now the one who has no fear. I will win my ant war. Someday.

Until then, practicing patience will come in handy for whatever bugs me or any other previously unmentioned display of arachnophobia.

FOR NEARLYWEDS

With the wedding pressure raised a few notches, in what ways do you find yourself getting under each other's skin? Is there possibly a bigger issue that's being ignored at the expense of arguing over minor annoyances? What irritations need to be resolved before they balloon into bigger issues?

FOR NEWLYWEDS

How have you annoyed one another in the past week or month? Talk about how you handled the conflict and what you learned from it. Instead of trying to change your husband or wife, how can practicing patience make a difference in your personal character and your marriage? (Be specific about what the issue is.)

You Cannot Say Whatever You'd Like to Say

17

Macho does not prove mucho.

—Zsa Zsa Gabor

A marriage without restraint is like a 747 without landing gear. I don't know about you, but I like landing gear. Especially when I fly on airplanes. Landing gear minimizes my need for a personal flotation device should I ever hit a large body of water at four hundred miles an hour. Landing gear gives me a sense of security, a confident feeling that I won't be launched like a crash-test dummy through pretzels and ginger ale and into some rich lady's glass of sparkling champagne in first class. Unimpeded by Dom Perignon, landing gear will keep my body from careening forward, exploding into the cockpit unannounced, and straining through the aircraft's instrument panel like Play-Doh, where in a liquefied state, I would quickly leak out of the plane at thirty thousand feet and rain gooey gobs on the Heartland of America, my left eyeball landing on Grandpa's corn on the cob at the Fourth of July church picnic.

I like landing gear. It gives me the hope for a new tomorrow.

A lot of fights in the first couple of years of marriage get started because many newly married couples underestimate the necessity of the critical concept known as *restraint.* Many well-meaning couples wrongly assume that they can say whatever they think or feel without regard to how their new spouse might receive the intended message. This simply isn't true, nor is it wise.

I think honesty, like landing gear, is a good thing. It's always the best policy, but in marriage, every policy comes with certain terms and conditions. That's why knowing how and when to use restraint is critical to landing potentially explosive conversations. Communication restraint will keep you and your spouse from launching each other into the emotional stratosphere. As a personal test dummy, I will illustrate the important concept of communication restraint and how it relates to air travel and married life.

On a recent trip home from Cape Cod, I had to fly from Providence, Rhode Island, to La Guardia airport in New York. From New York, I had to catch a flight home to Orange County using my "e-ticket." My initial response to using my e-ticket was, "Cool! I thought Disneyland stopped using those things a long time ago!" It was a rude awakening when I discovered I wouldn't be traveling home via the Pirates of the Caribbean. I was going home via Dallas/Fort Worth.

My travel agent told me that my e-ticket had one stop.

From Providence, La Guardia was supposed to be my first and last stop.

My Dallas/Fort Worthless e-ticket meant two stops. One too many. Back in high school, I was horrible in geometry, but one of the few things I remember is that the quickest way to get somewhere is to draw a straight line between two points, or something like that. Dallas/Fort Worth added a third point, a very southerly point, to my itinerary. That's not exactly what I call direct, but who am I to complain? I'm just the customer.

What I wanted to say to my geometrically challenged travel agent was . . .

I'll be sure to get right on that Kennedy assassination the moment I arrive in Dallas, right after I dig a few oil wells and strike so much black gold I'll be filthy rich enough to buy my own jet so I won't need these blasted e-vil-tickets, but not a minute before I rope and brand four thousand longhorns before sundown. Yee-haw!

Instead, I practiced communication restraint.

Before I got on the plane in Providence, I sat on the floor at Gate 20 for two hours because La Guardia was fogged in. Soon, my bottom felt like it'd been shot up with Novocain. So, I started to do some stretches. On the floor, I threw my right leg over my left leg like I was playing a solo game of Twister. I was minding my own business when an older lady sitting nearby commented to her husband, "Oh! Look at that stretch. Now that's a good stretch!"

Inspired by my Gumby athletic prowess, she stood up and began practicing tai chi movements. Like a graceful swan, leaping tiger, or cabbage egg roll, she went through a series of movements that reminded me of an electric mannequin. I could tell she wanted me to comment on her graceful tai chi moves and maybe, possibly, even join her. Not in a New York minute.

What I wanted to say to Mrs. Tai Chi Pokémon Karaoke was . . .

Hisss . . . ssstay back Pot Sticker. I am e-ticket Cobra, and my venom will drop you quicker than you can sing "Deep in the Heart of Texas." You marvel at my slithering stretches, but I've been sitting on the floor for two hours, and my bum is very sore. I've already had a two-hour drive, the lady at Dunkin' Donuts put three scoops of sugar too many in my coffee, and I'm being sent to the Lone Star State against my wishes. I'd watch my Happy Trails if I were you.

Instead, I practiced communication restraint. I smiled politely and went back to my stretching without a word.

When I arrived at the Big Apple, I dashed off the plane and sprinted to another terminal to catch my flight to the Wonderful Land of Rawhide. My plane was leaving in minutes, and I didn't have a second to waste. I sprinted for my gate and almost had guns drawn on me when I approached a security checkpoint. I threw my briefcase and travel bag onto the x-ray machine conveyor belt, which was moving close to the same speed of a first-time maid of honor walking down the aisle.

I zipped through the walk-through electric scanner and reached out to grab my bags. Seeing I was in a rush, the security guy picked up my bombcase, I mean briefcase, and said, "Do you mind if I look in your briefcase?"

Almost out of breath, I said, "No, but I'm about to miss my plane."

What I wanted to say to Mr. Save the Big Apple from Terrorism was . . .

Why don't you just say it? I look like a terrorist, don't I? Don't just check my briefcase, check my travel bag too! It holds more explosives and AK-47s than my briefcase does. While you're at it, why don't we do a strip search right here in public? I've got nothing to hide. Seeing that our national security's at stake here, I'm ready to bare all!

Instead, I practiced communication restraint. The guy was just doing his job, keeping innocent travelers from making their connecting flight to places they didn't want to go. I understood where he was coming from.

I spent forty minutes of my life deep in the heart of Texas and reboarded the plane to an interesting scenario. As we were taxiing toward the runway, an unruly two-year-old two seats forward refused to sit down and buckle her seat belt. She screamed like someone trying to find a human on the other side of a voice-mail system, and her parents couldn't get her to settle down. A young flight attendant hurried down the aisle and said in an urgent voice, "Excuse me, honey. What's your name, sweetheart?"

The flight attendant's innocent question ignited a flurry of seat kicking, flying fists, and high-pitched screams so loud you'd think someone smuggled a wounded mountain lion on board.

"Brittany. Her name's Brittany," the exasperated mom said.

Ever so confident in her flight attendant training, the flight attendant said in a direct, authoritative voice, "Brittany. Listen to me,

Brittany. You need to buckle your seat belt because if you don't I'm going to have to take you forward to speak to the captain."

More mountain-lion screams, only this time with fangs and claws bared.

"That is not going to work," the mother deadpanned.

"No, you don't understand, ma'am. If there is an incorrigible passenger on board, the captain will stop the plane and make her disembark."

The flight attendant was obviously single. No experience with *los niños.*

What I wanted to say to Ms. One Child Psychology Class in Junior College was . . .

Give it a rest! You are obviously making this situation worse than it is, which leads me to hope we don't have a real emergency on this flight. Go back and get the kid a cookie, a coloring book, and a staple gun to nail her to the seat. "Don't make me stop this airplane" was a nice try, but you can't reason with tantrums or terrorists.

Instead, I practiced communication restraint. The poor flight attendant was doing the best she knew how. Wait until she has children of her own. She'd better buckle in tight. Really tight.

By the time I arrived in Orange County at 5:30 P.M., I was exhausted from a long day of travel and so much communication restraint. All I wanted to do was see my wife and get tackled by my four kids. When they greeted me in the hallway at John Wayne airport with a colorful sign that read "Welcome home, Daddy," I was all the more thankful for landing gear.

TOGETHER FOREVER

You'd never think of taking off or landing in a plane without buckling your seat belt, would you? You'd hope that your pilot would remember to lower the landing gear before making his final approach, wouldn't you? You'd think that now that you're married you'd be able to say anything you want, whenever you want, to your new spouse as an expression of truth, sincerity, and honesty, wouldn't you?

Marriage is not a place where you can say whatever you want when you want, because some things, even though they may be honest and true, can also be hurtful and harmful to your marriage if not said in the right way. Like a 747 careening down a runway without landing gear, careless words can leave a lot of burning wreckage on the same runway that's designed to send your marriage soaring to new heights.

Guys are always told to work on being good communicators. That is one of the chief tasks of husbandry. Therefore, a newly married guy, by being honest, thinks he's keeping the lines of communication clear with his new bride. In his mind, he's doing their relationship a favor by giving his wife unsolicited feedback on her culinary capabilities. His words are the cooking tool equivalent of a verbal Ginsu knife.

"Honey, was your mom a prison chef? This goo tastes like penitentiary pasta."

A perfect example of a 747 attempting to land without landing gear.

Husbands aren't the only ones guilty of verbal flybys. It's not uncommon for a young bride to help dress her new husband so he will look like a presentable member of society. This can be a point of particular contention, especially if a guy has been used to his mom dressing him all his life.

"No dear, you cannot wear all black. We are not going to a funeral, and you are not Johnny Cash. This party is going to be fun and festive, so why don't you put on the outfit I laid on the bed for you that matches my dress?"

Is this why Norman Bates, Jason Voorhees, and Freddy Krueger are sworn bachelors?

Every day, you're presented with all sorts of situations in which you might like to say exactly what's on your mind to your spouse.

Instead of mincing words, dancing around the subject, or feeling like you're walking on eggshells, it'd be so much easier to just blurt out exactly what's bugging you at the moment.

"Don't you ever watch Tide commercials? Whites and colors don't mix!"

"This is a toothbrush. It's used to combat halitosis and morning breath."

"Unpaid bills have late fees! Did you hear me? I said late fees!"

"You will not wear that outfit if you want to be seen with me tonight."

Saying the right thing in the right way is like buckling in for a safe airplane trip. It makes you and your spouse feel safe enough to say what you both need to say in a way that lifts your relationship instead of grounding each other to separate terminals. Communication restraint, like a seat belt, secures your tongue when you hit unexpected turbulence in your marriage. It keeps both of you from getting thrown to the ceiling with words that are best left unsaid.

Though you and I will inevitably say the wrong thing at the wrong time in the wrong way more than once or twice throughout our married lives, what's the best course heading toward watching what you say in married life? Here's a flight plan that will set your marriage in the right direction.

Be an Encourager. If you want to have your wedding cake and eat it too, the best in-flight meal you can serve your husband or wife is a generous amount of encouragement. Given daily, encouragement will give your spouse the courage, strength, and stamina to fight whatever the world throws at him or her. There will be plenty of times in the days ahead when your husband will walk through the front door feeling like his job nailed him like a two-hundred-pound spitball. Your wife may be more beautiful than Ariel the Little Mermaid, but there will be days when she feels uglier and bigger than Ursula the Sea Witch. Discouragement. Insecurity. Doubt. The mounting pressures of work and life can beat up the strongest of spouses.

That's why your spouse needs encouragement. Encouragement is a wonderful gift to give to your spouse. It is a deep cup of water for a thirsty, discouraged soul. Encouragement is something everyone needs, but you can only get it when someone gives it to you.

My wife is a great encourager. From time to time Krista will tell me, "I really appreciate how hard you work for our family." Other times she'll say something as simple as, "I'm so thankful to have you as my husband." When I hear encouraging words like these, I'm reminded of who's most important to me and why. Krista's encouraging words make me want to return the same thoughtful words to her. A friend of mine calls encouragement "giving someone a verbal bouquet of flowers." I like that. Encourage your spouse, and they receive a verbal bouquet of flowers. The right words at the right time can create a beautiful bouquet that will last long after your wedding day. Make it your goal to encourage your husband or wife daily. Encouragement is always in bloom.

Practice Gentleness. Marriage isn't anything like adolescent development. There are no training bras or athletic supporters. There are no practices or dress rehearsals. You get engaged. You have the wedding. *Boom!* You're married—now get along for the next fifty years. That's why practicing gentleness is absolutely necessary not only in the first year or two of marriage, but throughout all of married life. You will make mistakes. Your spouse will make mistakes. Growing together in your marriage is a process, and gentleness is one of the most important character qualities to making a good marriage great.

Say the first thing that comes to mind, and you'll usually regret it. Wait a few minutes, a few hours, maybe even a few days, and you'll come up with a better choice of words to help your spouse understand what's on your heart. Blurting out leads to blowups, but gentleness can give you the perspective you need to respond in a way that resolves conflict instead of escalating it.

Honor and Respect One Another: It's always easier to point out your spouse's character flaws, bad habits, or shortcomings than it is to look inside and see what you need to work on yourself. Instead of saying whatever you want whenever you want, make it your goal to honor and respect your spouse before anything or anyone else. When you honor and respect each other as a husband and wife, that says a lot about who you are as individuals. It says a lot about your character and personal integrity. It says a lot about the sincerity and authenticity of your love for one another.

So how do you honor your spouse? How do you show respect to your husband or wife in a way that makes them feel like you're his or her number one cheerleader? Whether you are a husband or wife, you esteem the other person's role and the important part he or she plays in your life. You value your spouse as an individual, and you value his or her unique thoughts, ideas, gifts, talents, abilities, preferences, desires, wants, and needs. You esteem the unique contribution your spouse makes in your life and in the marriage you share together. You don't disparage or belittle your spouse in public or in private. You deal with issues directly, handling one conflict at a time. You affirm your spouse for who he or she is as a person and the unique qualities he or she possesses. You offer your spouse plenty of grace and space to grow at his or her own pace, as you both work on making your new life together the very best it can be. Do these things, and you'll see your marriage come together forever.

Be an encourager. Practice gentleness. Honor and respect one another.

This is what every marriage needs for a perfect three-point landing.

FOR NEARLYWEDS

How do you encourage one another in your relationship? In which area of your life do you need to practice more gentleness? Give a few practical examples of how honoring and supporting one another strengthens your relationship.

FOR NEWLYWEDS

In which area of your life do you need more encouragement right now? When you're on the verge of a conflict, how can practicing gentleness help you resolve the problem more quickly? Describe what a marriage looks like when a husband and wife honor and support one another. How can you do that today?

You Know It, and You Just Can't Deny It

18

To keep your marriage brimming,
With love in the loving cup,
Whenever you're wrong, admit it;
Whenever you're right, shut up.
—OGDEN NASH

When newlyweds begin to live together in holy matrimony, it doesn't take long for holy matrimony to be punctuated with occasional moments of unholy acrimony ("bitterness or ill-natured animosity, especially in speech or manner," *American Heritage Dictionary of Minor Marital Annoyances and Spats*). Unholy acrimony occurs when one not-so-well-meaning spouse fails to take responsibility for his or her actions.

This is a newlywed no-no.

Thus, a major marriage developmental task for newlyweds is taking responsibility for one's actions. To ensure peace, harmony, and goodwill in the marriage relationship and to prevent the hurling of derogatory insults like *Inconsiderate Pig, Nitwit, Toad Wart, Scum Face, Pachyderm, Three-toed Sloth,* and *Spineless Bottom Dweller,* it is essential to admit fault for slight oversights, forgetfulness, errors, omissions, blunders, flounderings, and botched attempts to hopelessly defend yourself for wanton irresponsibility. Persistent failure to take responsibility for one's actions usually results in a measurable spike in the relational Richter scale, producing red-hot, poisonous volcanic language that is not suitable for print in a book read by couples who are, literally, madly in love.

A flash point, or moment of marriage malfeasance discovery made by a mildly irritated spouse, like the failure to replace an empty roll of toilet paper with a new one, is usually followed by a loud, rhetorical yell from another room in the overly dramatic fashion favored by pretentious lawyers as seen on TV. The marriage malfeasance can be due to any number of newlywed first-year faux pas, many of which are related to household duties and chores, but not limited to other errors and omissions such as:

"Who mixed the whites with the colors?"

"Who left their dishes in the sink?"

"Who stuck an empty milk carton back in the fridge?"

"Who didn't wipe the water off the sink counter?"

"Who didn't hang up their bath towel?"

"Who left the coffeepot on?"

"Whose turn is it to clean out the cat box?"

"There's nobody in this room. Who left the light on?"

"Who sprayed for ants and didn't wipe them up?

"Who dumped their clothes on the floor? Mom's not here to pick 'em up!"

"Who didn't flush the toilet?"

"Who left the garage door open all night long?"

"Who forgot to pay the bills this month?"

"Who tracked mud onto the new white carpet?"

"Whose turn is it to make the bed?"

"Battery's dead. Who left the dome light on in the car?"

"Who left the toilet seat up?"

"Who forgot to lock the door before they left?"

"Who didn't call their mother back and tell her we can't make it Saturday night?"

"Who left cracker crumbs all over the couch?"

"Who forgot to pick up my dry cleaning for my job interview tomorrow?"

"Who promised to make dinner tonight?"

"Who didn't write it on the calendar?"

"Who lost the remote by not putting it back on the TV where it belongs?"

"Who didn't return my repeated calls from work?"

"Who took the last five dollars out of my wallet?"

Once the marriage malfeasance has been brought to the Offending Spouse, who is guiltier than sin, excuse me, innocent until proven guilty, the Offending Spouse begins to exhibit the psychological manifestation of a particular trait often identified in the FBI profiling of serial killers and telephone solicitors who refuse to take no for an answer. It is the suspension of reality known as *denial.*

If you suspect that your husband or wife is manifesting the sneaky symptoms of denial for failing to take the trash out at night so the task will fall on your trash day tomorrow or if you repeatedly discover smelly socks on the floor like skunk droppings in the forest or hard-water deposits on the shower door from the wombat who willfully doesn't wipe the water off the glass, here is a helpful acrostic for identifying an Offending Spouse in utter D.E.N.I.A.L.

D: Desperation manifested in deliberate defensiveness.
E: Egregious omission of error and evidence.
N: Negation of new and noteworthy offenses in addition to primary offense.
I: Inability to offer a shred of evidence to substantiate one's innocence.
A: Absolute abscondence in accepting accountability.
L: Loathe to lose a battle already lost.

Once the Offending Spouse has been cornered like a bleeding, wounded bobcat with rabies, the calm, logical, rational, and reasonable mild-mannered spouse who's "Simply asking a question" must prepare for the battle he or she ignited with the accusatory torch of truth. Maybe newly married "friends" of yours have had a conversation or two like this . . .

Prosecutor: All right, who put the cheese in the fridge without a Ziplock?

Offending Spouse in Denial: Not me.

Prosecutor: Oh yeah, well it wasn't me. I don't eat cheese.

Offending Spouse in Denial: Well it wasn't me, so don't blame me.

Prosecutor: I wasn't *blaming*. I was *asking*.

Offending Spouse in Denial: I eat cheese, so you implicated me when you asked, *(nasal tone)* "Who put the cheese in the fridge without a Ziplock?"

Prosecutor: Those lazy, irresponsible, self-centered MICE!

Offending Spouse in Denial: Go ahead and say what you really think.

Prosecutor: You put the cheese in the fridge without a Ziplock! And you left the Wheat Thins box out on the counter! And you put the knife in the sink without washing it off and putting it in the dishwasher! You know it, and you just can't deny it!

Offending Spouse in Denial: Did not!

Prosecutor: Did too!

Offending Spouse in Denial: Prove it!

Prosecutor: *YOU ARE A GUILTY, GUILTY, GUILTY LIAR!*

When it comes to occasionally not taking responsibility for dishwashing duties, colors versus whites mix-ups, trash-day takeouts, mother-in-law miscommunications, returned phone call forget-me-nots, toilet flushing flukes, gourmet dinner reneging, remote controls under the couch, and lost toothpaste cap crises, husbands and wives are equal-opportunity offenders.

Husbands live in denial.

Wives live in denial.

You know it, and you just can't deny it.

Since I've been married longer than you, I have no qualms about admitting a few of my malfeasant marriage behaviors that drive my wife crazy. I have nothing to hide, no need to be dishonest, and no need to live in denial. It wouldn't matter anyway. When Krista knows that I know I'm wrong, there's nothing I can do to deny it. And so I can proudly say that . . .

I'm the one who drains the milk carton until there is one fluid ounce remaining and then places it back into the refrigerator. *It's not empty!* I'm the one who places the toilet paper roll on the roller *incorrectly.* I like to tackle the tissue from the back of the roller. Hey, what can I say? I like a challenge. I'm the one who, instead of starting a new load of wash, leaves wet towels on the washing machine until they get that moldy, mildewy smell. I'm the one who grabs the bed sheet, the down comforter, and the bedspread from Krista's side. I tightly wrap it around my body and roll in the other direction, leaving Krista to sleep in her pillowcase. I'm the one who says, "Okay, we gotta get that car in to be serviced. Meet me at the dealership, and I'll bring you home." So, Krista shows up at the dealership while I'm sitting here at this computer typing away about how newlyweds can learn from my malfeasant marriage ways.

But for all my malfeasant marriage ways, Krista and I go mano-a-mano with what she knows she does and just can't deny. Krista isn't the Washer and Dryer Wonder Woman her friends think she is. I have pink BVDs to prove it. When the Pest Control Muse strikes her, Krista will occasionally spray for ants, but she doesn't wipe them up. "I sprayed the ants, so you wipe them up," is her insidious insecticide logic.

Krista is also Mrs. Stuffus Maximus. When we have company coming over and the junk mail, papers, bills, receipts, coupons, school artwork, miscellaneous wads of nothingness, ad infinitum are piled up on the kitchen counter, instead of either putting them away or throwing them away, she grabs the whole pile and stuffs it on the shelf in a nearby cabinet. Instead of going for pile *elimination,* she opts for pile *relocation.* Like the realtors in our hometown, Krista is a *relocation specialist.*

In our home, like many other guys, I'm in charge of taking out the trash. But the one thing that drives me crazy is when Krista and our four other malfeasant offspring pile high the kitchen trash can until it's overflowing with coffee grinds, eggshells, juice cans, soggy school papers, and a famished family of rats gnawing on El Pollo Loco chicken bones. "Can't *someone* place a new trash bag in the trash container so we're not playing kitchen soccer with all the refuse overflowing onto the floor?" I pronounce in a loud voice to any nearby adult over thirty and related to me by marriage who might hear me in the adjoining rooms of our home.

What *newlywed no-no* have you committed this week?

C'mon, you know it, and you just can't deny it.

TOGETHER FOREVER

Marriage is the celebration of being chosen, but it's also the place where you're gonna get caught. You can run, but you cannot hide from the long arm of your true love. When you casually forget to clean up the mess you made in the kitchen or when you dropped the ball by failing to fulfill your promise to wash the car because you were glued to the TV set watching your alma mater lose the big game over a fumble, you can either take responsibility for your fumble or get clotheslined by the opposition who's just calling 'em as she sees 'em.

Once you're married, you cannot live in close quarters without the common conflict of one person getting miffed by the other person not taking responsibility for something he or she did or didn't do. If you want to have your wedding cake and eat it too, that includes rinsing the crumbs and icing off your dessert plate and sticking the silverware in the dishwasher. It includes taking responsibility for your part in whatever has caused the current conflict you're arguing over.

But what do we mere mortals usually do when we get caught?

We defend. We deflect. We deny.

You and I know that we do this, and we just can't deny it.

We hate getting caught, and we hate being exposed or reminded of some areas of our lives in which we fell short. We didn't like getting caught as kids, and we don't like changing some of the very comfortable habits we've grown accustomed to like an old sweatshirt. Marriage has a laser-beam way of challenging and exposing our malfeasant mess-ups. But, instead of owning up and fessing up, we'd prefer to hold a full-length mirror up to our spouse and say, "Oh yeah, if youse tink dat I gotta problem, well taka luksee in da mirroar fer yer-self."

Having your wedding cake and eating it too isn't always easy. At times, in fact, it's downright difficult. That's why taking responsibility for your attitudes, actions, and words requires the indispensable character trait of humility. Humility is the one virtue that's always extolled but never really wanted. Think of Mother Teresa. A saint. World famous for serving the poorest of the poor. Humble? Without a doubt. Esteemed? Beyond measure. Any takers? Not too many.

Humility is an elusive character trait because once you think you've got it, you probably don't. If, in some way, you do possess humility, there's probably an upcoming opportunity in your immediate future to demonstrate it in your marriage when it'd be a whole lot easier to tackle the problem with a hefty helping of good, old-fashioned selfish pride. Humility costs us our comfort and our predisposition toward power trips. We'd rather pull on the boxing gloves than lay down our foolish pride.

Instead of defending ourselves with an overflowing garbage can of excuses when we forget to pick up our mother-in-law at the airport, humility says, "You're absolutely right. I'll get to the airport right away. Tell her I'll try to make it by sunrise." Rather than deflecting a spurious attack on our bathroom-cleaning disability by pointing out the date, time, and place of our spouse's most recent peccadillo, humility responds with, "That shower scum is relentless! You watch, I'm declaring war on shower scum." And instead of denying the obvious fact that our clothes, once they come off our body, do not stand up and walk to the closet by themselves, humility says, "Okay, I'll work on picking up after myself."

Having your wedding cake and eating it too requires a healthy dose of humility because, like it or not, married life inevitably produces marital strife by exposing our shortcomings, faults, sins, weaknesses, character flaws, stinky habits, and our proclivity for making a prideful declaration of denial that any of the aforementioned characteristics exist in our lives. Humility is healthy because it helps your marriage grow past the gunk that gets in the way of enjoying one another, which is the exact reason you got married in the first place.

So when you're arguing over who forgot to make the bed or who forgot to pay the rent, how do you put humility into action?

Give Up. A lot of the more simple problems or conflicts can be avoided in marriage if one person gives up ground to the other. Instead of manning your battle station, you give up your need or desire to be right. Refusing to defend, deny, or dig into your position doesn't mean you're going to be a doormat for your spouse to stomp on, because real humility operates from a position of inner strength, not weakness. Giving up may also mean choosing not to point out a glaring error you see in your husband or wife, or if something has been pointed out to you, giving up mounting a heated defense. Giving up, when done for the right reasons, is simply knowing what is a silly or insignificant issue that's not worth fighting over.

Own Up. When you mess up, be a Latin lover and declare *mea culpa.* When it's your fault, just say so for crying out loud. I know it sounds so simple, but for some people, taking responsibility for their actions is a major challenge because it's so much easier to point out someone else's mistakes and weaknesses. But searching for flecks of sand in your spouse's eyes when you're packing a sequoia tree in your own does not promote feelings of goodwill and harmony in any type of relationship.

Instead of giving your spouse a performance review, take your own personal inventory and see if anything is missing on your shelf. Taking responsibility for your actions is a major marriage developmental task for newlyweds and not-so-newly married couples alike. This life is filled with choices, and our choices have positive or negative consequences. Marriage is a day-by-day, minute-by-minute reminder that our choices have an impact on our spouse and family. Be humble and own up. Take responsibility. Say you're sorry. Humility is healthy, and you've got some alternative medicine coming to you if you think differently.

Make Up. If you're the kind of person who likes to see other people grovel and squirm for forgiveness, *get over it*. When your husband or wife has given up or owned up, don't come at them with a self-righteous battering ram by saying, "Ha! I knew I was right all along! What would this world do without people like me who stand for justice and common decency? I knew you'd finally see the error of your ways."

Defending, deflecting, and denying aren't very good problem solvers, but there's nothing worse than hanging forgiveness over someone's head like a dog going after a bone.

Here, Skippy, you want the bone? You're gonna have to jump for it. C'mon, Skippy, you can do it! Higher, Skippy, higher!

Selfish pride has an "in" door and an "out" door.

Humility goes both ways.

Don't manipulate a confession or capitulation by threatening, victimizing, pouting, or giving the silent treatment. Forgive your spouse. Nobody likes a self-righteous, pigheaded hard-nose. You didn't marry a bovine, so don't act like one.

Look Up. Some of the stupidest fights in newly married life have nothing to do with toothpaste caps or trash cans. Sometimes we have the tendency to react all over each other because we don't know how to put into words what's really bothering us. When you catch yourselves arguing for the fourth time over why the bath towels were not folded in the fundamentally correct fashion, ask yourselves, "Is this the real issue here? Are we really fighting about bath towels or is there a bigger issue we're both not seeing? Is the real issue control? Or independence? Or fear? Or frustration? Or doubts? Or insecurity? What are we really fighting over?"

Look up at the bigger picture of your marriage and see if there's a larger issue that needs to be addressed. And when you look at the big picture, look to God to give you wisdom and insight for how to handle the inevitable conflicts that happen in married life. Look to God for strength. For perspective. For forgiveness. For freeing yourself of the need to defend, deflect, and deny. For humility. Even if you don't know what your marriage is going through, God knows, and He won't deny you the privilege of asking Him for help. He's the One who's going to help you stay together forever.

His help is just for the asking. God knows we all need it.

FOR NEARLYWEDS

What habit can you get away with now but won't be able to when you get married? (Be honest!) Identify four to six major areas of responsibility that are essential for a good marriage. Why is accepting responsibility critical to making a marriage work?

FOR NEWLYWEDS

What is something you both do that drives the other crazy? In which areas do you have a tendency to point out each other's mistakes? If your spouse is going to point something out that you did or said, how would you prefer to hear the bad news? How can humility make a practical difference in owning up and extending forgiveness to one another?

This Is Not What I Had in Mind

19

Most women are introspective:
"Am I in love? Am I emotionally and creatively fulfilled?"
Most men are outrospective:
"Did my team win? How's my car?"

One of the happiest days of my engagement to Krista was the day I discovered my favorite sporting-goods store had a wedding registry.

"Yes!" I pumped my fist. "This is a major score!"

Imagine how thrilled I was to be one of the first grooms to participate in selecting sporting items for the home. Not that I didn't have a say in the other two dozen bridal registries Krista had signed up for at every major department store, home store, boutique, and AM/PM gas station minimart in Southern California.

Oh, I did have a say all right.

Like other guys about to be married, I just didn't have a vote.

Bridal registries are for brides, not for grooms; any guy who thinks otherwise is in for a rude surprise should he decide to join his bride-to-be on a wedding registry jaunt and try to cast his vote. Choosing the china dishes, silver settings, crystal glasses, linens, bed skirts, pillows, blankets, shower curtains, bath mats, guest towels, bathroom towels with matching scented toilet-paper rollers, flatware, cookware, Tupperware, underwear, kitchen utensils, carpet, drapes, candy dishes, serving dishes, hydraulic forklifts, napkins, those doily things, all appliances from blenders to toasters, and the exact same kind of dishwashing detergent used by her mother are the exclusive domain of your bride.

What's really amazing is that all of these items will match.

If you're lucky, you'll get to pick out the ironing board.

When I found out that Sports Chalet had a wedding registry, Krista and I hopped in my Land Cruiser and zipped down there as fast as my former bachelor vehicle would go. When we walked inside, I was practically salivating.

Now I know what it feels like to be a woman!

Before me stood aisle after aisle of amazing athletic merchandise that never in my wildest dreams could I ever afford by myself. I was going to pick out exactly what I had in mind. Exactly what I had envisioned that would make our marriage the active, fun, fit marriage I dreamed it would be. I got to pick out my, I mean *our,* own gifts. I was so excited, I didn't know what department to start in first. This was better than Christmas!

After our wedding, when it came time to open all of our wedding gifts, I felt like I had married and gone to heaven. Here's the booty that I (there I go again), that *we* brought in: climbing rope, climbing gear, down sleeping bag, North Face tent, two Thermarest sleeping pads, two-burner stove, Lowe backpack, two fanny packs, and too many other assorted athletic items to mention at the risk of making my newlywed guy readers weep at their missed opportunity *TO SCORE BIG TIME LIKE I DID! YEAAHH!*

Sorry. Don't mean to rub it in.

But after all the weddings gifts for hearth and home have been opened and the newlyweds begin to settle into married life, an amazing thing happens. The bride and groom received almost every wedding gift they registered for. The home is shaping up to be the nice little nest the bride had envisioned. Those shiny new plates and vases look so clean and fresh on the newly painted kitchen shelves. Those expensive silver settings that ignited more than a few big fights between penny-pinching husbands and the gift-conscious, receipt-hiding wives who gave them are in the china hutch and will be brought out once every decade. The matching bathroom towels and bedroom linens look like they jumped out of the Martha Stewart Camouflage Catalog. Everything a newly married couple dreams of having in their home to start their new life together has come together. It's exactly what they had in mind.

Everything is perfect.

The only problem now is the marriage.

The marriage is not turning out like what the bride and groom had in mind.

Newlyweds who experience the natural phenomenon of post-wedding buyer's remorse (i.e., Can I trade my husband in for a formal tea setting at Nordstrom? Will Sport Chalet give me a portable basketball hoop for my wife?) are usually reluctant to voice any stress, struggle, or recent near-strangling in their marriage because it was only a short time ago that they stood before gazillions of family and friends to profess their undying love for one another. When newlyweds make that sudden shift from marital bliss to marital blisters, they usually first confide in a trusted friend who has trod the marriage path a bit longer than they have.

For guys like John and Newlywed Ted, shooting hoops is a good place to start.

John: So how are you and Jenny doing? Coming up on your first anniversary, right? *Ka-THUNK!*

Ted: Uh. Yeah. Hmm. Well. Has it already been a year? Good thing you reminded me. *Ka-THUNK! Ka-THUNK!*

John: Don't want to be missing the first one, Kemo Sabe. You miss the first anniversary, and you'll hear about it for every anniversary to come. So how are you and Jenny doing?

Ted: Yeah . . . right, uh, we're doing okay.

AIRBALL . . . no sound.

John: Sounds like trouble in River City?

SWIISSH!

Ted: Okay, so what's the deal with women and sex? *Ka-THUNK!* We didn't make love the other night because I forgot to do the dishes. What is up with that?

John: I see we've struck a nerve. Welcome to Leonard Nemoy's *In Search Of . . .*

Sorry to interrupt the conversation, but while John is coaching newlywed Ted on the fine art of shooting baskets and wooing a wife who wants the dishes done before serving a helping of herself, Jenny is sitting down at a coffee house with Allison, John's wife. A sixteen-year-old girl with purple hair and 4,381 pieces of metal in her body, one of which is a soup ladle pierced through her tongue, stands at the cash register waiting to take their order.

Allison: Jenny, you're going to absolutely love the café mochas here. *(To the iron maiden)* Give me a nonfat, decaf café mocha, light on the foam and lots of sprinkles.

Jenny: I'll have the same, but make mine a double, caffeinated, grande, no foam, and throw in one of those huge chocolate-chip cookies.

Metal Mouth: That'll be sixteen-fifty.

Jenny and Allison wait for their drinks and find a quiet place to talk.

Allison: John can't stand it that I spend more money on these coffee drinks than he spends servicing his car. But what can I say, he has to love me for who I am, right?

Jenny: I wish I could say the same about Ted.

Allison: My, my, my. Not too happy. Is he complaining he's not getting enough sex?

Jenny: *Yes!! That's exactly what he's complaining about! How did you know?*

QUICK CUT TO JOHN AND TED

Ted: I was doing *so good.* I was on my best behavior. I did every thing she asked me to do, but then I forget one little thing like doing the dishes, and she says that's the straw that breaks the camel's back. What am I . . . her personal pack mule? *Ka-THUNK!*

John: (Laughing) Welcome to married life. *SWIISSH!*

QUICK CUT TO ALLISON AND JENNY

Jenny: And then he got mad at me for feeling sad and disappointed and hurt and frustrated that he didn't have the simple consideration to do what I asked him to do.

Allison: You didn't nag him, did you?

Jenny: No! I did not nag. I asked nicely.

BACK TO JOHN AND TED

Ted: And then she starts in on me about my mother. Oh boy, did we stir that pot!

John: But don't you dare say a thing about her mother! *Ka-THUNK!*

BACK TO ALLISON AND JENNY

Jenny: And then . . . and then . . . he said the most terrible thing about my mother. I shot back, "What does you not doing the dishes have to do with my mother?"

Allison: Wrong question. Never ask a question you don't want an answer to.

FINAL TAKE ON JOHN AND TED

Ted: So I said, "Your father always did the dishes. Well, I'm not your father!"

John: So what kind of flowers are you planning on bringing home to Jenny? *Ka-THUNK!*

FINAL TAKE ON ALLISON AND JENNY

Jenny: I'm not saying sorry till he says sorry. And he'd better bring me roses.

Allison: A wise strategy.

TOGETHER FOREVER

If you've thought about your marriage lately and said to yourself, *This is not what I had in mind,* then rest assured: You are not alone. If you've wanted to trade your husband or wife in for the new-and-improved version, you are not alone. If you blasted to the moon and beyond with wedding-day elation and the honeymoon sensation of being in love forever only to crash and burn upon reentry into the reality world of the earth's atmosphere, you are not alone.

The postwedding blues of disappointment and disillusionment are a normal part of the newlywed experience.

Think about it: You and your new spouse have just expended huge amounts of physical and emotional energy to blast off into married life. You are now in a completely new place than you were three to six months ago. Being husband and wife changes who you are, who your spouse is, and how you view and relate to one another. Upon entering married life, you also brought with you all sorts of ideals, dreams, expectations, and ideas of what you thought married life would be like. When you start to hit the inevitable hiccups, speed bumps, and conflicts that all newly married couples are prone to argue about, *it's completely normal and natural to feel disappointed and disillusioned.*

It doesn't matter who you are or what kind of family you came from—all men and women enter marriage with marriage ideals that never seem to match the real picture of day-to-day married life. When your ideals don't match the reality of what you're experiencing, it's easy to feel like your marriage is going down the tubes when it barely got off the launch pad. Like a lot of newlyweds, what you have in mind about marriage before you enter it and your ideals about how married life should be are more often tied to damaging marriage myths than to a realistic, balanced perspective of what marriage really is. The newlywed couples who experience the least amount of disappointment and disillusionment in the first few years of marriage are those who have a realistic expectation of love and marriage. If you want to have your wedding cake and eat it too, you need to be willing to sort through the marriage myths that all too often pose as wedding-day ideals. Once you understand how damaging these myths and unrealistic expectations can be to your marriage, you and your spouse can work on changing your perspective so you can focus on the marriage principles that will help you enjoy one another so your marriage will stay together forever.

Myth 1: Married Couples Who Really Love Each Other Don't Fight. Aw c'mon! Ask any couple who you know loves each other and have been married for a long time, and they'll show you the boxing ring they just built in their new room addition. *Couples who really love each other are the best fighters.* All couples disagree, argue, fight, squabble, nitpick, battle, brawl, struggle, scrap, and whine at each other with the utmost pugnacity. The real trick to going mano a mano with your mate is knowing how to resolve your differences so you can move on to making love, not war. Conflict resolution is a key stay-together-forever principle that every marriage needs. Since conflict is a part of every marriage, handling conflict in marriage means learning how to fight clean and fair by not throwing low blows. And most important, you have to know how and when to end a fight with plenty of forgiveness.

Myth 2: Sex Will Be a Snap. Not getting it all the time like Ted? Tired of a *slam-bam-thank-you-ma'am* husband who falls asleep 2.3 seconds after making love? He wants sex, and she wants romance? Just as you can experience a lot of relational conflict in your first year or two of marriage, you can expect sexual conflict too. Sex is another form of marriage communication, and if you're having problems verbally communicating, it's only natural that those problems will show up in your sexual relationship. Sex is not a snap. Sex is a mystery wrapped in layers and layers of myths, many of which we see daily in magazines, commercials, and movies.

Some couples are sexually compatible and others aren't, but sexual tension will always be a part of married life. Like any other aspect of your marriage, it takes work to have a healthy sex life. You have to be able to communicate to your spouse what you like and what you don't like, what's pleasurable and what's not, what you need and when and how often. In all that, you have to learn how to compromise and to learn what leads your spouse to feeling wildly amorous.

Myth 3: We Will Know How and When to Meet Each Other's Needs. Wrong again! If we humans knew how and when to meet each other's needs, then we would never have *conflict!* It's precisely because we don't always know how and when to meet each other's needs that we experience disappointment and disillusionment in marriage. I can only meet Krista's needs when I know exactly what they are, and she can only meet my needs when she knows exactly what they are. The only problem is that our needs change from day to day and week to week. And even when I know what Krista's needs are, does that mean I eagerly want to meet her needs all the time? No way! I get selfish. I like my comfort zone. I want her to meet my needs first.

See where we're going here? Couples who have their wedding cake and eat it too are those who learn how to consistently communicate their needs and mutually work together to meet each other's needs in the best loving, unselfish way possible. There's just no other way to make a marriage work.

Myth 4: We Will Always Feel in Love. Where's Barry Manilow when I need him? Hit it, guys!

"Feelings! Whoa, whoa-oh-oh feelings!"

You will not always feel in love.

There. I said it.

You do not always feel like going to work. Or taking out the trash. Or paying taxes. Or getting expensive dental work. Where in the world did we ever pick up this myth that marriage means we will always feel in love? Nibble on this one for a while.

Myth 5: God Will Protect Our Marriage. Some newlyweds naively believe that because they got married in a church with special prayers and blessings and because they both love God, God will automatically shrink-wrap their marriage with a special dose of anticonflict gunk that will protect them from all the temptations and slimy opportunities for sin in this world.

Survey says? BZZOONKK! Wrong again!

If you want a realistic picture of having your wedding cake and eating it too, the best place to look is in the Bible, because that is where God clearly says what He has in mind for how a husband and wife should love and respect one another. God gives us the freedom to make our own choices, and if we allow Him to work in our lives, He will empower us to be the very best husbands and wives we can be. God will protect your marriage as you yield yourselves to how He says to obey Him and His Word. He'll allow you to face temptation, but He'll always provide a way out. The choice of receiving God's protection is His free gift to your marriage and your relationship to one another. And that will happen through the struggles, strain, disappointments, and disillusionment that are a part of the growing process of learning how to be married and persevering through every problem you encounter to stay together forever.

If you've been disappointed and a bit disillusioned with how you thought married life would be, hang in there. Maybe it's time to reevaluate your ideals and see if they were myths that won't do your marriage any good. Once you figure out where you are, talk about it with your husband or wife. Don't minimize, hide, or try to mask your feelings for what they are. You just might be on the verge of one of many new breakthroughs and insights that are an integral part of learning how to have your wedding cake and eat it too.

Go easy on yourself and your new spouse. Marriage is a lifelong process of learning and relearning how to love one another in a deeper, more meaningful way.

Register that in your heart and mind, and you'll never want to take it back.

FOR NEARLYWEDS

Which of the five marriage myths do you identify with the most? Why is it so important to have a realistic picture of marriage going into it? What needs have you identified and communicated to one another that will be an important part of your marriage?

FOR NEWLYWEDS

What disappointments have you experienced so far in your marriage? How have you had to realign your ideals and unrealistic expectations? Take some time now and talk about how to meet each other's needs and how to develop healthy expectations for where your marriage is today.

The Big Move

20

Don't overanalyze your marriage. That's like yanking up a fragile indoor plant every twenty minutes to see how its roots are growing.

I'm dead tired of moving. As the son of a funeral director, I grew up with all sorts of different-sized boxes lying around the house, but the next box that gets moved out of my house, I'm gonna be in it.

In the time we've been married, Krista and I have made four major moves. Across town. Okay, so we haven't moved across the country or to Guam, but I don't care if we're talking about moving next-door, a move is a move, and it takes a lot of work to get me in the groove to move. I realize moving only four times may seem like relatively few moves compared to people in the military or those who are fleeing from the local authorities, but for a guy who'd rather go surfing or lie on the beach reading a book or making sandcastles with his kids, moving ranks right down there with standing in line at the Department of Motor Vehicles, which usually takes longer than your average move. Moving also ranks way down low with trying to get a referral from any HMO organization that works with humans. Well, maybe not. Moving doesn't kill most people unless a refrigerator falls on your face, but you could die from a common cold before getting a HMO referral.

I am all moved out. I'm staying put.

Laguna Niguel. Capistrano Beach. Laguna Hills. San Clemente.

We've made four moves within ten square miles, and I'm tired of feeling like a human pachinko ball. I tell you this because during the next five to ten years, you, too, will probably make a number of moves. I am preparing you for the upcoming moves you'll make and how to make a smooth transition from one apartment with a leaky roof to a new condominium that shares a wall with a sixteen-year-old boy who just received a drum set for his birthday to finally the day when you move into your own single-family home that will provide you with the joys of home ownership, large bills from Home Depot, and far more chores on the weekend than you ever did as a kid.

You're going to make all sorts of moves as a couple. When you buy a new condominium, remember that buying a condo has nothing to do with birth control. Or you may move across country to take a new job where, for all you know, you will live next-door to a nice old man who likes cats, classical music, fine wine, leisurely walks, but just so happens to be on the FBI's Ten Most Wanted List. Some of you are high-rolling, risk-taking, wealth-building newlyweds who don't have a large enough down payment for a new home, so you'll roll the dice by playing Internet stocks on-line. Before you know it, you'll be moving backward and into your parents' homes for buying stock in sucker.com. Or, after saving and saving and/or getting some hefty help from the folks, some of you will be ready to plunk down a deposit for a brand-new home with brand-new friendly neighbors in a brand-new neighborhood that sits on top of a major earthquake fault in a flood plain which fronts a definite hurricane path that also happens to be a touchdown sight for killer tornadoes because the closest trailer park is ten miles away. But that shouldn't matter—you should see how the bathroom wallpaper matches the living-room carpet.

If you and your new spouse are planning on moving anytime in the next year or so, Krista and I have some very strategic ideas about when to make your move. Since moving involves a ton of work and can be very stressful on a marriage, we say you go for it and make your move as complicated as possible. Ratcheting up the difficulty of a major move is a guaranteed stress test to see just how strong your marriage really is. Be like us and . . .

Only move three weeks *before* Christmas.

Only move three weeks or five weeks *after* having a new baby.

With four kids, we applied this last principle twice, which means we're batting .500 for learning how to inflict the highest amount of stress on our marriage as possible.

The final idea for making your move as complicated as possible should only be applied once, because once you apply this principle, you'll vow over your pet chinchilla's grave that you'll never do it again.

Begin packing for your move on the day of your move.

Krista and I had only been married a year and a half when our first move came—three weeks after our first child was born. We were moving from one condo to another condo, where I'd just spent the past two weeks painting and scraping wallpaper, the most wicked form of home-improvement grunt work known to guykind. I painted the entire place with not one, but two coats of paint. Krista was a new mom consumed with feeding, changing diapers, and waking at all hours of the night. We'd both been really busy, so moving day just sort of jumped out at us like a U-Haul van outta nowhere.

Come moving day, Krista and I were emptying whole drawers into boxes. Just pouring them in the boxes like pouring water into a bucket. No detail. No organization. It's as if the United States had just been invaded by a foreign army, and we only had a couple hours to pack all of our belongings to flee the country. Our friends pulled up in a truck they had borrowed and came to our front door.

"You guys all ready to go?"

They looked around our half-packed condo and said, "What have you two been doing?"

A better question might have been, "What have you *not* been doing?"

So if you're dying to pack and move on the same day, just double the time it'll take, triple the stress you'll endure, and alienate your friends who will never help you move again in their lives.

Many newlyweds look to cut down on their moving time and expenses by selling all the worthless junk they accumulated as single adults and all the useless wedding gifts that they couldn't trick a department-store employee into taking back. I'm all for garage sales because garage sales give you keen insight into how ridiculous your spouse can really be. Garage sales show you exactly what your spouse thinks is most important in this life. Garage sales are also a great way to start a fight, which, if couples are open to learning new conflict-resolution skills, can be a great opportunity to practice how to successfully negotiate and compromise. Negotiation and compromise are absolutely necessary marriage skills for any couple who wants to cash in on the lucrative garage-sale circuit. Before a garage sale can take place, a husband and wife first have to agree upon what constitutes a garage-sale item.

Wife: You really don't want these old Bruce Springsteen CDs, do you?

Husband: The Boss stays. Those'll be worth lots of money some day.

Wife: You can't be serious. Hey, those are mine!

Husband: I say we dump Madonna and Duran Duran.

Wife: I like Duran Duran! "Her name is Rio and she . . ."

Husband: Okay, keep your VH-1 pretty boys. Let's get rid of this old candy bowl.

Wife: That was my grandmother's candy bowl! I can remember sticking my fingers into that candy bowl every Christmas when I was a little girl. No way!

Husband: C'mon, sweetheart, we gotta compromise. We can't keep all this stuff.

Wife: Okay, I'll give up the candy bowl if you get rid of all those old smelly sweatshirts.

Husband: Smelly sweatshirts? Those are my NFL game-day shirts!

Wife: Four smelly sweatshirts for one candy bowl.

Husband: One candy bowl for two smelly sweatshirts!

Wife: Three smelly sweatshirts for one candy bowl and one *Duran Duran's Greatest Hits.*

Husband: You got yourself a deal.

Wife: Now what about this old baseball-card collection? You never even look at these things.

Husband: Don't even go there!

TOGETHER FOREVER

Moving day is always unpredictable. You never know what's going to get broken, scratched, or dinged. Moving day is one of those days where we guys are tempted to use our bowling words. We wonder how in the world the couch we're carrying ever made it up that teeny-tiny stairwell obviously designed for leprechauns. The items you tell yourself and others not to scratch are the ones that get scratched. The unbreakable objects are the ones that get broken. The things you really don't care about are the things that make it through the moving journey without a hitch, and the things you really do care about are the things that get thrashed. Moving day is the day when every one of Murphy's Laws comes tumbling out of the truck.

Moving day is a lot of work, and so is keeping a marriage moving in the right direction. When Krista and I were first married, we asked each other what kinds of attitudes and actions would keep our marriage moving in the right direction in order to keep it from falling off the truck. As we blasted off into the wild world of wedded wonder, we wanted to be sure to keep moving and growing in the same direction. Like planting a garden, we wondered what kinds of seeds needed to be planted in order to bear long-term fruit so we could stay together forever. We knew the seeds we wanted to plant early on in our marriage may not sprout or bear fruit in the first few years, but with a lot of work and laughter along the way, maybe those seeds would eventually make our marriage something special. Which seeds would produce fruit in five years? In ten years? In fifteen years? Twenty years? Forty and fifty years? If we worked on growing and moving in the same direction together, could we really have our wedding cake and eat it too?

To have your wedding cake and eat it too so you can have a together-forever kind of love, your marriage requires your very best time and attention. Marriage is a constant process of attending to and managing your relationship. You have to water it, feed it, weed it, prune it, and harvest the fruit that grows. You will reap what you sow, but if you pack your life full of marriage-distracting activities, overcommitments, and misplaced priorities, your marriage is going to get choked by the weeds of lesser things.

Though our first few years together went pretty smoothly, as we continue to move forward in our marriage, life has become increasingly difficult and more complicated. It's not that we haven't experienced a lot of joy, laughter, thankfulness, and love along the way, but we've also struggled a lot from losing a job at a church where I worked for seven years, worrying over finances, experiencing the deaths of loved ones, and dealing with the day-to-day battle of painful chronic tendonitis I have in my wrists from being a full-time writer. Even the greatest of marriages have times of struggle and hardship, and that's why I think the character qualities we've talked about so much in the book have got to be in the center of our hearts if we really want to have our wedding cake and eat it too.

As you move into the groove of married life, you'll soon discover that living together, staying open to communicating and flexing with one another, trying to negotiate and compromise, learning how to resolve conflict, balancing work and home priorities, creating a home together, having children, managing finances, and dealing with the challenges that life throws your way will not simplify your life, but all these things will complicate your life. That's just the way life is, but if you work at keeping your priorities straight, you'll discover all the joy and love you need to keep your marriage together forever.

If you're going to make your marriage the wedded wonder God designed it to be, you'll need to constantly work at it. In the crazy pattern of life, there are going to be times when work does take over, when the kids do drain all of your energy, when sickness does consume your attention, when sex isn't a snap, and when finances frustrate you, but through all these different challenges, make your overriding commitment to work at your marriage because marriage is worth every single ounce of time and energy you put into it.

So the challenge before you is to keep your marriage on course by moving and growing in the same direction so you can stay together forever and enjoy all the wedding cake that each day brings you in your life together. And when you wake up each morning, remember to dress your heart with God-given qualities so you can be your best for the one who wears the wedding ring you gave as a symbol of your together-forever love.

> Therefore, as God's chosen people, holy and dearly loved, clothe yourselves with compassion, kindness, humility, gentleness and patience. Bear with each other and forgive whatever grievances you may have against one another. Forgive as the Lord forgave you. And over all these virtues put on love, which binds them all together in perfect unity. (Col. 3:12–14)

Dressing your marriage for success with the character qualities we've talked about and growing together in the same direction can only happen as you each make the time to do those things that make your marriage work. Too many people long for love, but they're not willing to work. I guess you could say a poor work ethic is tied to *a poor worth ethic.* Too many couples suffer from lousy, frustrating marriages because they value their spouse and marriage like a cheap garage-sale item.

Just how valuable is your new marriage?

How much do you love and cherish your new spouse?

Are you really willing to go the distance and do whatever it takes to stay together forever? You can only have your wedding cake and eat it too by having a high worth ethic for your spouse and your marriage. Love, honor, value, treasure, and serve your spouse, and you'll have so much wedding cake, you won't know what to do with it all!

When marriage is good, it's really good. Nearlyweds and newlyweds, you have so many wonderful moments ahead of you that you'll look back on your first few years together as priceless, valuable treasures, so make your move today and be the best husband or wife you can be. Sure, you'll goof up and make mistakes along the way, so remember to be generous with tenderness, compassion, and forgiveness. Above all else, don't ever lose the incredible gift of laughter given by the One who can boogie on the dance floor of our lives like no other. You see, in God's eyes, every day is moving day, and there's nothing better than sliding into bed after a long day's work and snuggling next to the one you love. Be thankful for the simple joys like that, and you'll discover the wonderful secret of having your wedding cake and eating it too.

FOR NEARLYWEDS

What will keep your marriage moving and growing together in the same direction? What is a practical way to show this week how much you value your fiancée?

FOR NEWLYWEDS

Where have you found it easiest for your marriage to get knocked off track? What quality can you work on today that will make the most difference in your marriage? How can laughter and being thankful for one another help your perspective when your life and marriage get complicated?

Have Your Wedding Cake and Eat It Too!

A PRIMER

HOW NEARLYWEDS AND NEWLYWEDS CAN STAY TOGETHER FOREVER

We started this book by blasting into the wild world of wedded wonder, and I hope you've had as much fun as I have. As you begin your new life together forever, here are a few short reminders on how to do just that. Be sure to revisit these ideas and principles every few months to make sure your marriage keeps moving and growing in the right direction. There's nothing better than having your wedding cake and eating it too with the one you love. Dig deep into your love, and remember to keep your hearts centered on God's love as you enjoy all the wonderful gifts He freely gives us each and every day. Go ahead and pig out. After all, *it is your wedding cake!*

1. Together-forever couples are willing to laugh, learn and work in their marriage.
2. Together-forever couples take the time to talk about how their upbringing influences how they think, feel, and act in marriage.
3. Together-forever couples dress for marriage success by wearing God-given character qualities.

4. Together-forever couples are extremely committed to one another.
5. Together-forever couples choose each other every day for the rest of their lives.
6. Together-forever couples are intentional and purposeful in marriage planning.
7. Together-forever couples work on how they communicate with one another.
8. Together-forever couples do the money dance by making wise financial choices.
9. Together-forever couples don't underestimate the power of sin and selfishness.
10. Together-forever couples wear lingerie and offer lots of emotional intimacy.
11. Together-forever couples work at understanding each other's family differences.
12. Together-forever couples are willing to grow, learn, and change for one another.
13. Together-forever couples establish clear marriage-bed rules.
14. Together-forever couples support and challenge one another in a healthy way.
15. Together-forever couples make their marriage first by creating boundaries for in-laws.
16. Together-forever couples kill ants together by dissecting the problem, not the person.
17. Together-forever couples encourage and practice gentleness by honoring and respecting one another.

18. Together-forever couples take responsibility for their attitudes and actions.

19. Together-forever couples examine marriage myths to overcome disillusionment.

20. Together-forever couples move and grow in the same direction so they can have their wedding cake and eat it too.

About the Author

Joey O'Connor is a conference speaker and the author of twelve books for couples, parents, and young adults. He lives with his wife, Krista, and their four children in San Clemente, California, where he likes to surf, eat fish tacos, and lie in the hot sand.

His works include:

I Know You Love Me, but Do You Like Me?
How to Become Your Mate's Best Friend
Women Are Always Right and Men Are Never Wrong
In His Steps: The Promise
You're Grounded for Life and 49 Other Crazy Things Parents Say
Heaven's Not a Crying Place: Teaching Your Child about Funerals, Death, and the Life Beyond
Excuse Me! I'll Take My Piece of the Planet Now
Whadd'ya Gonna Do? 25 Steps for Getting a Life
Breaking Your Comfort Zones
Where Is God When . . . 1001 Answers to Questions Students Are Asking
Graffiti for Gen X Guys by J. David Schmidt with Joey O'Connor
Graffiti for Gen X Girls by J. David Schmidt with Joey O'Connor

For speaking events, conferences, and seminars, call (949) 369-6767. You can also write to Joey O'Connor at P.O. Box 3373, San Clemente, CA 92674-3373. Visit Joey's Web site at *http://www.joeyo.com* or e-mail Joey with your comments and questions at *joey@joeyo.com.*

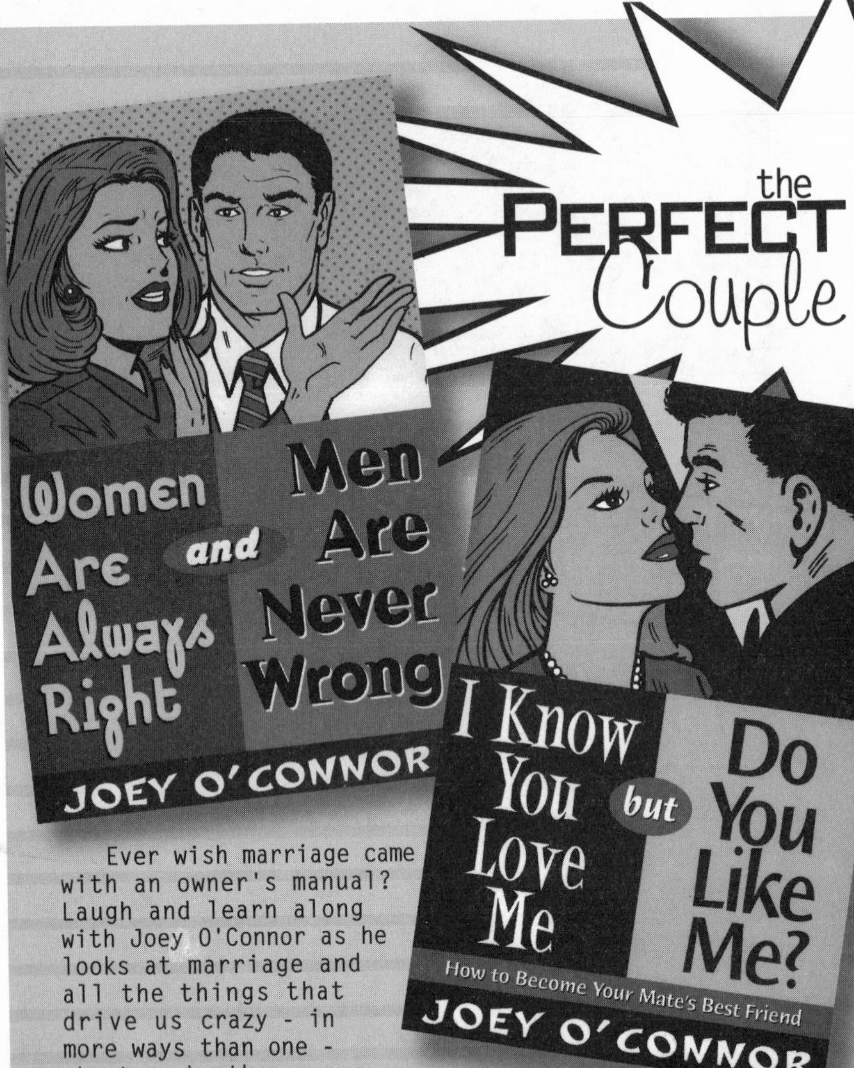
the PERFECT Couple
Women Are Always Right and Men Are Never Wrong
JOEY O'CONNOR
I Know You Love Me but Do You Like Me?
How to Become Your Mate's Best Friend
JOEY O'CONNOR